CRACK
IN THE ARMOR

CRACK
IN ARMOR
THE

A POLICE OFFICER'S GUIDE TO SURVIVING POST TRAUMATIC STRESS DISORDER

An inspirational true story by
JIMMY BREMNER
with **CONNIE ADAIR**

Foreword by
Sgt. Mike Babineau, retired

Canada

Published in 2010 by
Bremner Associates Inc.
6A-170 The Donway W. #1915
Toronto, ON
M3C 2E8
Canada
www.bremnerassociates.com

Library and Archives Canada Cataloguing in Publication
Bremner, Jimmy, 1959-
        Crack in the armor : a police officer's guide to surviving post traumatic stress disorder / Jimmy Bremner with Connie Adair.

Includes bibliographical references and index.
ISBN 978-0-9866957-0-4

1. Bremner, Jimmy, 1959-. 2. Police psychology. 3. Police--Job stress.
4. Post-traumatic stress disorder--Patients--Canada--Biography.
5. Police--Canada--Biography. I. Adair, Connie, II. Title.

RC552.P67B73 2010   616.85'210092
C2010-905458-X

Cover design: Simon Truong and Olivia Truong
Inside design and formatting: Yee Truong
Cover image: Marko Shark

Printed in Canada

Transcontinental Printing

To
Dayle, Michael and Kacey

To my brothers and sisters in
blue and their families in the hope
that this book will provide an
inspiration on their journey to wellness

Contents

Foreword

By Sgt. Mike Babineau

Special Weapons Team One, retired

A brief silence on the radio was broken by the familiar voice of the police dispatcher. "Pioneer Donuts. Dundas and Jarvis. Man with a shotgun."

This could not be happening, I said to myself. I had just seconds ago left the donut shop and everything was in order. "Sergeant 52, I'm on scene," I advised the dispatcher.

I entered the shop knowing that there was no man with a gun. He would have had to have come in as I was going out, I was that close. But I would check and advise.

The frantic owners met me as I entered. In a mix of English and Chinese, they managed to tell me that someone had been shot in the bathroom and that they had locked the door from the outside, trapping the shooter and his victim inside. This was a call for SWAT.

Moments later a group of tactical officers arrived, led by a constable who, even though he was of the same rank as the rest of the team, was obviously in charge. Like a maestro conducting a symphony, he directed the team, putting them in strategic positions, making decisions on the fly and gathering crucial intelligence until, as if rehearsed, they moved as one and entered the room. Both suspects were brought out in cuffs. One had beaten the other but neither had been shot.

The team was Special Weapons Team One. The officer was Constable Jimmy Bremner.

This was the first of what turned out to be many encounters I would have with Jimmy and the team. It was the beginning of a friendship that would grow with the passage of time – a bond that we have shared for almost 20 years, the type of bond that can only form between two people who have shared the same experiences, felt the same pain, laughed together, cried together, fought together and played together. Brothers-in-arms.

Eventually Jimmy and I would work together on the same team. Special Weapons Team One was an eclectic group of individuals, each with their own special qualities blended to make a team that would raise the bar of excellence.

Crack in the Armor is a must read for any and all emergency responders and their families. In it Jimmy Bremner chronicles his fall from grace as an elite team leader and a member of the country's largest SWAT unit to alcohol abuse, living on the streets and attempting suicide. The road to recovery from Post Traumatic Stress Disorder is one that must begin at the bottom. There is only one direction – up. Up or die. This book also tells the story of Jimmy's climb back to health and to the top as a sought-after lecturer.

With the help and support of many, Jimmy has turned his life around and reaches out to those in positions where the disorder is most likely to strike: emergency responders.

Introduction
By Connie Adair

The first time I met Jimmy Bremner, in 2009, we sat huddled in the basement of a huge house in Mississauga, whispering so we wouldn't be heard as an episode of the television series *Flashpoint* was being filmed upstairs.

Jimmy, the show's tactical police consultant, explained how he helped train the cast to portray members of an elite team, based on Toronto's Emergency Task Force, showing them how to hold weapons correctly and to work and move as one. More importantly, he shared stories with them about his experiences as a SWAT team leader and the emotional realities of responding to more than a thousand calls so the writers and actors would be able to depict the team realistically.

Actors Hugh Dillon and Enrico Colantoni, who portray sniper Ed Lane and Sgt. Gregory Parker, arrived decked out in full tactical gear, ready for their next scene. They spoke highly of Jimmy and joked with the man who had given them insight into a world so unlike their own.

Jimmy stood, quietly confident, clearly respected by all in the room, a man totally together. So it was with surprise that I learned of the difficult journey he had made from alcohol abuse and attempted suicide to a life that is successful, both professionally and personally, and full of hope.

Jimmy joined the police service in Toronto at the age of 26 and spent the first three years as a general constable. In 1989, he became one of a select few officers chosen to join the SWAT team. That had been his goal from the time he joined the force.

He loved being on the job, putting every ounce of energy into making arrests, and loved being a member of the elite SWAT team. He responded to about a thousand calls, many weighing heavy on his mind and heart as he bonded with the people he negotiated with only to watch as they took their own lives when they couldn't be talked down, or when they became aggressive and threatened life and he had to shoot them.

However, the high point of his career, working SWAT, soon enough became his lowest point as he developed Post Traumatic Stress Disorder as the shootings and exposure to violence continued. He also lost several family members within a relatively short period of time.

He was troubled but he felt there was nowhere to turn. Asking for help, he thought, would make him appear weak, something not tolerated by others on the job. Instead, he turned to drink, hoping it would make sleep come easier, and later, hoping he would pass out and not wake up at all.

Jimmy went from SWAT team leader to waking up on the street following repeated drinking binges. Eventually a fellow officer found him in a car on the shoulder of Highway 401, passed out and with a gun.

Jimmy started to see clinical psychologist Dr. Sean P. O'Brien and about six months later was admitted into a mental health and addiction centre.

Two months of treatment were followed by years of struggle, and highs and lows that would take him from feeling like,

"Is recovery worth it?" to the happiness he felt as he put his family life back on track and started to share his experiences with PTSD.

Jimmy told me he wanted to tell his story in hopes of letting other police officers know Post Traumatic Stress Disorder is an illness and there is no shame or weakness in being ill, and no crime in reaching out for help. *Crack in the Armor* is his take on things as they happened, containing his thoughts and advice based on his experience. He shows how important it is to realize PTSD is an illness and should be treated as one. He says the cop mentality of being afraid to ask for help must be broken.

Crack in the Armor tells of the events that led to his breakdown and includes entries from his personal journal chronicling his time in rehab, a time he would not have fully remembered otherwise.

Many times Jimmy felt helpless as he fought for his life, sometimes day by day, other times hour by hour.

Jimmy shares his struggle to become whole and to manage the stress of awaiting the verdict of impaired driving charges. He was convicted and went a year without his licence. He says having to walk everywhere, although humiliating, gave him time to think. Almost a year later, the conviction was overturned and he was acquitted.

Eager to start a new chapter in his life, Jimmy decided to share his experiences at conferences and with support groups, and to help any officer who needs it.

Dr. Sean P. O'Brien, an authority on police officers and PTSD, has contributed a chapter, *The Doctor Says,* about the medical side of the disorder.

A Note from Home, by Jimmy's wife, Dayle, reminds officers not to forget about the effects that PTSD can have on their families.

In *A Note from the Sergeant's Desk*, Sgt. Mike Babineau tells of the difficulties he faced in helping his colleague and friend, and the heartbreak of watching his downward slide.

In *A Call for Change*, S/Sgt. Barney McNeilly, retired, president of the Canadian Critical Incident Inc., speaks candidly about the need to recognize and tackle PTSD in the police workplace and the changes that need to be made.

In *A Note from the Writers' Desk*, television series *Flashpoint* co-creators/writers Mark Ellis and Stephanie Morgenstern describe how Jimmy's experiences have shaped the award-winning police drama.

I hope Jimmy's story gives you the strength to fight and to know there is life after Post Traumatic Stress Disorder. You are never alone. There is help and hope.

1

"I shot the man I was talking to only a minute before. The team performed by the numbers and we had executed a hostage rescue. The doctor and the baby were unharmed. I picked up his firearm to clear the weapon. It was a pellet gun."

The Beginning of the End

I joined the force in Toronto in 1986 at the age of 26, old for a police officer. I had studied and worked in the graphic arts field but was always fascinated by the police and military. Graphics work was like being a musician – there wasn't a lot of money. So when I married and needed to provide for my family, it was time to choose a new career. Policing seemed a natural thing to do. I didn't, and still don't, like seeing people being pushed around, and I wanted to protect people who couldn't protect themselves. As cliché as it was, I joined the force because I wanted to help people.

When I first started the job, I was highly motivated. I was assigned to a busy downtown division where a lot of the people were victims, driven to crime to buy what they needed to get through the next day. Some officers see things in black and white, people as good or bad. I never could.

I never had trouble arresting career criminals, but when it came to people who were emotionally disturbed, the line between right and wrong became blurred. Typically these individuals were unresponsive to reason. I will never understand how one small person with no training could hold off six tactical officers. This usually resulted in injury to my teammates and me, as well as to the subject in question. But medicated, that same person would be as gentle as a lamb. I guess the feelings I had for those individuals was that they lacked intent.

When you deal with society's worst one per cent, one hundred per cent of the time, it's not long before it begins to cloud your judgment. You begin to see everyone as a potential threat or puke. But now I see pukes as victims. They're people dealing with their own trauma. I don't see them as enemies.

I served as a general constable for three years. I had drive, which I inherited from my mother and grandmother. It has been both a blessing and a curse. Not long after I started and had a permanent partner, we started making more arrests than anyone in the division. One day the sergeant left the room and I was confronted by my fellow officers. They told me I arrested too many people and that I was making them look bad. I was baffled by their attitude.

Later I asked the staff sergeant what I had done wrong. He said, "Nothing." I knew I had to get out of there and it was then that I told him I wanted to get onto the tactical team. That had been my goal from when I first joined the service. I had no interest in being an investigator or riding a horse.

In the meantime, I was put on the quiet south end of the division. On the first night, I stopped a truck going the wrong way on a ramp. I ended up arresting one of the biggest construction thieves in Canada. It was a huge arrest, the kind an officer gets once every 10 years. It happened during the time when I was supposed to be lying low.

The day I was selected for SWAT duty couldn't come soon enough. I came to the team with only three years of patrol experience, which was unheard of. In my drive for perfection, and being highly motivated, it took me only 18 months to become a team leader.

I would spend the next 16 years with the team, as acting sergeant, explosive disposal member and training officer. When all was said and done, I probably responded to over a thousand calls for service.

During my years with the team, my drive got me into trouble again. My team of 10 highly motivated people took more serious calls and shootings than most. We injected ourselves into situations rather than asking, "Are we required?" If we saw a need for equipment and it was not provided, we went out and bought our own because we wanted to be professional. Many of those items are now issued pieces of equipment.

I couldn't stand to be mediocre and neither could my teammates. I have been told that a hummingbird's metabolism is so fast that it sees the world in slow motion. This is how I felt.

Some people say police work is 90-per-cent boredom and 10-per-cent panic. It can be boring if you let it get boring.

If you don't get out of your car and ask what's happening, when something happens and you don't expect it, you panic. I prefer to be proactive.

Operating at a high level presented its problems. When you're on, you're on, and when you're not, life goes by too slowly. My drive was a good thing if I could focus it; otherwise I would create problems, feeling better when there was chaos. Later in my SWAT career, I would go home and there would be nothing to do so I would drink. I didn't know why I was doing that then, but I understand it now.

When I started the job, I can remember saying during the interview, "I don't drink." Ten years into my time at SWAT, I was a proficient drinker. Drinking in policing is like a reward for doing a good job – like a dog gets a biscuit for giving a paw.

It was a work hard, play hard atmosphere, and the self-medication helped me to get over some tough feelings about the outcome of a number of troubling calls. I wasn't comfortable with all the violence. It was hard to come to terms with. During training we practiced handcuffing and naturally the subject complied. It wasn't the same in the real world. Obviously the guy we were arresting hadn't taken the same course. Instead of being cuffed without a fight, he would go crazy and be hard to get under control. This would mean an application of force, and force can't be applied without violence of action.

We could "win" situations, but still be traumatized. One call that stands out was at a condo by the lake. The killer was in the room and the door was partly open. I could see a guy lying there. He had been stabbed 50 times if once. It was a horrible scene. We entered and rescued the body while the killer was still in the apartment. I dragged the body into a stairwell and went back to clear the apartment. We located the killer under a bed. He was apprehended, so we were successful, but the victim was still dead.

After that shift, some of the guys were going for a drink. I thought why not? You deal with the worst 20 minutes of someone's life over and over. It adds up and turns into a series of bad memories, nightmares and flashbacks. Drinking helped me forget, at least for a little while.

At first the drinking was social, but it started to get out of hand. I found myself overwhelmed by my home life and the stress at work. Shift work takes its toll on family life. I couldn't talk to my wife. How can you come home after carrying a dead body then respond cheerfully when you're asked to put up a shelf? I didn't want to bring the horrible experiences home. It's not appropriate for a woman and kids to hear, so when asked, "How was your day?" I'd simply answer, "OK."

I didn't know then how important it is to have someone to talk to. If you can't unburden yourself, the stress gets bottled up and it can eventually affect your health.

In my time with the police service, I have witnessed horrible scenes of violence and brutality – dead or dying people of all ages, and homicides and suicides of all descriptions. The worst calls were the bloody ones and the suicides. The public doesn't know all that goes on in the night – the domestics that turn ugly, the hostages, the suicides. But I kept my feelings to myself, determined not to show any weakness. We hide by thinking, "It's part of the job" as if this somehow makes the brutality OK.

Similar to the Stockholm Syndrome, where hostages bond with their captors, I have found myself bonding with people while speaking to them through doors. One particularly memorable call involved a young man who had violently assaulted his girlfriend and barricaded himself in his apartment.

The team breached the front door and we made our way methodically through the apartment. The door of the last bedroom was barricaded. I spoke to the man for quite some time through the door.

The team then broke through the door and entered the room. A male was sitting cross-legged on the floor with his back to the wall, quite peaceful. The only thing wrong with the picture was that he had a 22-calibre hole in the centre of his forehead. That image would stay with me for a long time.

I don't know what bothered me more, the tragic way in which people took their lives or what seemed to be the cop idiom that we did all we can do and if he takes his own life, no worries. I'm not happy with "We've done all we can do." It seems like something losers say. Some officers spend their careers worrying about what would happen if they were to take action. I have always worried about what was inevitable if I didn't take action. Isn't it our job to intervene?

During the more than 24 years I was an officer, I became a changed person. I didn't want unconditional acceptance; I just didn't want to be judged by management or peers. If I was asked to do something, I would do it, but I didn't want to hear from an armchair quarterback afterwards. Second-guessing destroys unit cohesion. I wanted to feel as if the service supported me and had my back, but I began to feel that I was a problem for the organization and the harder I worked, the bigger the problem they thought I was.

However, for the most part, I seemed to be handling things fine. I held the team leader role longer than anyone prior to my joining the team.

But in the late 1980s my battle with the insidious illness Post Traumatic Stress Disorder began. My stepbrother was killed in a car accident. I had to go and ID the body and arrange the funeral. My grandmother passed in 1992 and I lost my mother in December of 1996. Her death was quick and quite a shock. She was only 60 years old when she was lost to ovarian cancer. My uncle died a short time after that.

I was an only child, raised by my mother and maternal grandmother. I never knew my father. He left when I was two and a half years old and I haven't had contact with him since. I had a tight bond with my mother and her death was devastating.

My stepfather, Frank, was in ill health, stricken with cancer a few years later. Frank, who my mother met when I was five years old, was an interesting guy. He was a military man who ran my four stepbrothers and me like we were in the military. He was kind of rough around the edges but quite gentle at the same time. I would spend time performing palliative care for him. It was very sad.

Of course I didn't tell the team and I carried on as if nothing was wrong. There was no time for feelings. I would have to be strong. People were watching me and I could show no weakness. Don't bring your problems to work and don't take your work home with you – that's the police cliché everywhere.

In 1999 the team was running like a well-oiled machine. In fact our team was the entry team many of the squads asked for when there was dangerous work to be done. Sometimes squads would wait until we were on duty and then plan their raids.

That same year, on May 21, my birthday, the team got the call that a prisoner had broken out of Kingston Penitentiary and had gone on a bank-robbing spree across Ontario. Information was received that Ty Conn, a career criminal, was holed up in a basement apartment in the heart of the city.

We set up quickly on the house. I could see the wanted male in the basement with a shotgun. He was pacing back and forth. He had a shaved head, no shirt, just jeans and bare feet. He was in good physical shape, lean but acting like he was strung out.

We made our phone call and I began to speak to him. I opened a side door and was confronted by the suspect pointing a shotgun at me. I was concerned but had good cover and the advantage of high ground. So we talked. I introduced myself as Jim and asked how I could help. We talked for 45 minutes. He said I could keep all the money he had stolen and the stolen car. I was three to four feet away from the suspect.

At one point he put the gun down and went for a glass of water. The action plan was to drop two stun grenades and I would enter with a teammate and deploy the Arwen, incapacitating Conn long enough for us to get physical control. The team executed a limited entry but failed because the suspect got back to his weapon. The team, led by me, could not move rapidly in the confined space. My Arwen jammed. My only option was my pistol, but I could hardly shoot the suspect to stop him from killing himself.

I instructed the team to retreat to cover. I spoke to Conn for another 15 minutes. He had the gun facing toward his chest and was talking to me. He was also talking to a reporter on the phone. From my position at the top of the stairs, I could see Conn's body heave back as the gun discharged. I entered the room, where I found him propped up in the chair. The shotgun was still held by one hand. The team entered to secure the premises and placed the suspect in handcuffs, which is our standard procedure.

The medics worked on Conn but pronounced him dead a short time later. I left the scene feeling like a failure, not being able to save the suspect from himself. I developed some empathy for his situation; at one point he stated, "You don't know what it's like," and I had to reply, "You're right. I don't." I can identify with most of the situations people find themselves in, having lived through similar experiences, but having to spend the rest of my life locked up in a prison would be a bleak experience. What is a good day at Kingston Penitentiary?

The team spent time talking of the evening's events, naturally over a beer.

The aftermath was complicated and I am quite sure it was the beginning of my downward spiral. The command was not happy that we made the entry. The armchair quarterbacking and second-guessing began. There was no acknowledgment of the team's courage.

A few months passed and we were answering run-of-the-mill calls – man with knife, man gone berserk, drug raids. It was now December 1999 and we were the duty team on New Year's Eve, the night the world entered a new millennium. The unit commander thought it would be wise to have three teams on duty that night.

We did all of our equipment checks and went on the road. At about 2130 hrs. we answered a man with a gun call. When we arrived at the address, we were met by a man with a lever action rifle. He was quite drunk. There was no drama in this call as the suspect collapsed drunk on the floor. We arrested him and made the weapon safe.

We were back on the road, with the clock getting closer to midnight. A call went out at St. Michael's Hospital in downtown Toronto. A doctor was being held at gunpoint. The gunman was demanding that his baby get immediate medical attention.

The team answered the call and it was confirmed that the suspect was holding the doctor prone on the floor and the baby was on the desk in front of him. I said, "Hi. My name is Jim. How can I help you work this out?"

We talked. Some time passed. The suspect said that the incident would be over by midnight. In fact it was just minutes into the new year.

The gunman was in a trance-like state. With an expression that was almost a grin, he announced, "I'm going to end this now." Aggressively and abruptly he moved toward the hostage on the floor. Concluding that the hostage's life was in imminent danger, a teammate and I shot the suspect in the head at a range of less than one metre. I shot the man I was talking to only a minute before. The team performed by the numbers and we had executed a hostage rescue. The doctor and baby were unharmed. I picked up the firearm to clear the weapon. It was a pellet gun.

Where I work, police service protocol is to separate the officers involved in a shooting, seize their weapons and clothing, and segregate them until they give a statement to a senior officer. So back at the station I sat minus my weapons and uniform, alone and in my underwear, cold and worrying about the other team members.

At some point I was taken home. My wife and children were away, having spent the night with friends because I was on duty. I began to drink.

It was about five in the morning and I continued to drink, trying to come to terms with having killed someone and thinking that I had become a killer. How was I going to explain this to my family?

Well, the media looked after that for me. A small article mentioning a hospital shooting appeared in the newspaper that day, and in the days and months ahead, the media frenzy would grow to enormous proportions. There were accusations that police had planted the weapon on the man, that racism had played a part in the shooting and that somehow police had arranged for the shooting to happen off camera. The family of the deceased man had threatened to sue. It took 38 days for the Special Investigations Unit (the civilian body that investigates incidents involving police) to clear the shooting. That was over but it was 18 months before the inquest was completed and the recommendations of the jury were announced.

We returned to duty the night of Jan. 3, which I

thought was too soon, but to refuse would have been a show of weakness.

We attended another hostage-taking incident in the early hours of Jan. 5, and a second suspect was shot. In this case the team fought for control of a pistol. The weapon discharged only inches between the suspect and my chest. My immediate concern was for my teammates as I was uncertain who was hit until I saw blood rushing from the suspect's lower abdomen. The individual was treated by emergency services and survived.

Two shootings in five days by the same team. It had never happened before and would be the team's downfall. There would be no second chance. The team would be broken apart, a move that was very detrimental to the emotional well-being of all of us. I was demoralized and humiliated. I was placed in the training office not because of my expertise but, I felt, as a punitive measure. The only thing the training section had for me to do was sort brass casings. I did, and watched while a new sergeant and team leader drilled the members. That was humiliating and hurtful. I did not receive a psychological assessment following the shooting and did not seek the help of a psychologist. I believe I would have benefitted from immediate psychological intervention.

Some part of me said don't quit so I knuckled under and took every opportunity to assist in the training of new members. However, since 1999-2000, a day didn't pass when I didn't think about the incidents and the break-up of my team. I became very angry. I would burst into tears for what seemed to be no reason. I would relive those events every day, for hours at a time, right, wrong or indifferent. My drinking increased in volume and frequency, and this pattern would continue for four years. I was filled with anger, rage, guilt and shame. It was too much for one person to handle.

I began to drink until I passed out because I couldn't stand what I had become.

One night, when I was a young officer, I picked a drunk up off the street. He told me he used to be a fighter pilot. I thought, 'Look at you. What a mess.' Then one day I woke up in the gutter and the light went on. Now I understand, I thought. This is what happens to people who have been traumatized.

I was having trouble with my marriage and children as I had become a bitter and angry person. I stopped going to family outings. I stopped sleeping in my bedroom and slept in the unfinished basement, oblivious to the cold concrete floor. I became totally isolated. The only way I could go to sleep was by consuming alcohol until I passed out. Sometimes I hoped I would not wake up. I would go to work with one or two hours of sleep. People only saw the substance abuse, not the stress underneath.

In 2004, my stepfather passed away. It was the tipping point. Five months later I would be found at the side of the road, drunk and passed out behind the wheel with my gun in the car. I had been in Belleville going over the nuts and bolts of the St. Michael's shooting with some tactical teams. At that time, four and a half years after the St. Michael's incident, I had had no psychological help. I didn't realize that talking about what happened was like reliving the experience. I didn't know at the time that I was traumatizing myself again and again. If I had been under the care of a psychologist, the talking would probably have been therapeutic.

After I gave my talk to the officers, I had some drinks and set off for home. At some point, I pulled over on the side of the highway and passed out. Fortunately a brother officer found me and took me into custody.

There had been occasions when I would place a gun to my head and think about pulling the trigger. If I had not passed out on that night on the 401, I may have succeeded.

Even after this frightening incident, I didn't want to admit that I needed help. My wife and doctor wanted me to go to rehab but I didn't think it was necessary. I was in denial. Mostly I didn't think I was worth fixing. I thought that I deserved to be feeling the way I was because I had done something wrong and that it was all my fault. Instead of going to rehab, I continued to drown the nightmares and stress in alcohol. I walked for hours. Sometimes I slept in the backyard or woke up in the gutter. This continued for another six months, until, after much prodding from my doctor and my wife, I gave in and went to rehab. I did it for them. I didn't believe it would help.

2

"I am prepared for anything they throw at me. Nothing they say or do will be as bad as my last five years. I control my life."

The Journey Begins

In early 2005 I spent two months at a rehabilitation centre, staying overnight during the week and going home on weekends. Part of the treatment was to keep a personal journal to record my feelings during the course of treatment. It was also a way to help relieve stress. I have included some excerpts, in italics, in what follows. Keep in mind that my perceptions are just that: my perceptions of my time in rehab. It was a time of great emotional turmoil and stress.

Upon arrival I immediately felt comfortable with the group as we toured the grounds and over the next weeks we settled into a routine. Days started with community meetings, where housekeeping issues were discussed. It was mostly bullshit, as I wrote in my journal. Days were occupied by crafts and horticultural meetings, discussing emotional safety issues and listening to psychobabble. We learned how to interpret our emotions and feelings, safe ways to deal with anger, and about medications and their effects on the body.

On day two I was hopeful. *Workout, run and weights. I will be in better shape when I leave.*

My wife, Dayle, and my son visited me the first week, making me miss them even more. I realized how much I loved them, and my daughter, and how much I wanted things to work.

I tried to stay in shape. After full days of group and individual sessions, I ran, lifted weights and practiced martial arts.

We learned how trauma impacts daily life and were given the emotional tools to deal with problems. I vowed to work on my self-worth and rid myself of shame and guilt. *Shame – how I feel. Guilt is something I have done.*

On weekends we got to go home, but not before coming up with a goal we wanted to achieve. At the end of the first week, my goal was to take my wife out for dinner and a movie on the weekend. This would be a big step for a PTSD sufferer – one of the symptoms is to withdraw from family life, and I had. But it was not to be. I could not make a connection with my family and ended up sleeping in the basement.

I also vowed to take part in group activities and stop beating myself up. *I will work on assertiveness not aggression. I have a place in the group. I am important. Good workout today. I will leave here stronger, mentally and physically.*

Later, in craft class, I made a ceramic frog. I used art as a distraction to keep troubling thoughts from filling my head.

During the second week, I felt sad and missed Dayle and the kids, *but I have to finish what I have started.* I don't know if I could have made it without Dayle's constant support.

I took a two-km run. Every day I lifted weights, showered, shaved and brushed my teeth. Small, routine personal grooming habits are often forgotten with depression and PTSD. It was a move forward.

Despite my vows to get stronger, not all was smooth going. The experience was like a roller-coaster, with emotional ups and downs daily, even hourly.

I thought I would be cured at the end of the program, but I soon found out recovery is an ongoing process.

On the second weekend, I had dinner with Dayle and the kids and went shopping with my son. I met my daughter's new boyfriend. I tried to participate in everyday life.

Back in rehab, I was told that I am a perfectionist, and cycle until I burn out. It sounded very familiar to me. My mother was the same.

The next weeks brought a series of emotions. I started to lose confidence. When my wife said she loved me, I felt I was not worthy. But I continued to *vow to be stronger mentally and physically when I leave.*

I was told I was making progress and that I was coming out of my shell. At the same time, I was having headaches and trouble sleeping.

I continued to have problems with self-worth, and the feelings of guilt and shame continued as I tried to cope with no longer being a part of SWAT. *I don't know what is going to replace the tactical team. I feel I have nothing to go on for. I have to find something to replace it with. Must find pleasure in simple things. This will be hard.*

The third week continued and my emotional self was still having problems showing feelings and putting them on paper.

I attended an evening class about returning to work, but it was more for people who have regular jobs. They don't know the shame of breakdown and how it is seen in police circles ... *They don't know how much emotional energy it takes to run a gun team and train people, or to have your life on the line every day.*

I worked on issues of guilt and shame and how to deal with the on-going violence I had been exposed to for over 20 years.

I took art therapy. The doctor running the class centred out my Godzilla-like sculpture as being too good for class because most everyone else painted stick figures with black paint. All were interpreted as people feeling depressed. I guess I didn't understand the concept. This made me mad and I felt I had failed the class. This brought out the need for drink but I went for a long run and hit the weights.

I don't understand. It seems that they want you to have feelings when you walk into the class but if I say I feel fine it's not good enough. I think if I feel good it should be acknowledged as would bad feelings. I came here to get better, not worse or develop a chronic problem that requires me to come back. Almost at bullshit tolerance level. Glad it is the weekend.

My goal for the weekend was to get back into my own bed upstairs. *My wife picks me up and it is evident that things won't go as I had hoped. She is still on about the drinking. This makes me disappointed because I can't change the past. I must live for the moment. She doesn't get it. So when we get home I end up sleeping in the basement.*

My doctor once said I wasn't an alcoholic, but that alcohol was a way I self-medicated. Regardless of the reason for my drinking, it took its toll. My son was 12 and a half and my daughter was 11 years old at the time I was in rehab.

I look at the kids and hope it has not been too hard on them. I wish I had done more with my son when he was younger, but that being said I do have the future to make it up to him. My daughter is non-confrontational and even wrote a message of hope on her website. My heart was broken when she stopped speaking to me. I would really like to take both kids camping this summer to try and make up for the time I have missed with them and of course I would like to spend time with Dayle, just the two of us. She is the only person I have left. I could not go very long without her. I wish I could make things right with her but so much has happened I am afraid I can't make it up to her. My wife has always been there for me. I feel I am not worthy of her love.

The start of week four and we learned how to understand the PTSD process and how it affects daily life. One of the group's members, a war vet, really opened up, telling how his partner had been shot in the head. On another occasion he had to amputate the arm of a small boy in order to save him. He felt bad about his actions. Another group member told of shooting a man while on an operation overseas and the trouble he was having coming to terms with it.

I heard one member of the group was leaving. *She was*

my friend. She was sincere and always had a smile on her face. I can't believe her boyfriend would try to kill her. There were memories of violence everywhere.

I phoned home and told Dayle I had arranged couples' therapy. She seemed happy that I had carried out this task. *I just want her to be happy with me. I feel at times that I have ruined her life. However she tells me she loves me. I just wish I could bring myself to feel safe when she tells me this. This weekend my goal will be to get back in my bed beside my wife.*

I seemed to be making sense of things, yet was still having a problem developing a sense of self and belonging.

In a class about trauma and bonding, I was told that I was addicted to the adrenaline rush and am more comfortable in chaos, and when I have none, I make it. This explains my drunkenness and my picking fights with my wife.

My doctors said they saw a big improvement in me. *I guess there is some hope after all. That being said, I still don't know who I am and have become a robot.*

Next morning I tried to explain how hard it was to make it through the day and to live without chaos. I don't want to be ordinary.

I had my first EMDR (Eye Movement Desensitization and Reprocessing) treatment, a type of psychotherapy used to help trauma-related disorders. By paying attention to outside stimulus, such as something moving back and forth, the patient can still recall a traumatic experience but the experiences seem less disturbing. *I thought I could hold out but I crumbled. This type of therapy is emotionally exhausting. Again I felt the need to drink but I sought comfort in the group and the urge passed.* Later I called Dayle and told her I loved her. *This is very hard for me to do. I am starting to make the connection that I am afraid if I get close to someone they will abandon me. This is why I am emotionally cold and distant.*

I continued to have problems with being ordinary. I had to run and work out to get me through the craving to drink.

I also wrote in my journal regularly. I was starting to enjoy writing about my day. *I will leave here stronger than I arrived. I will get better. There is too much to lose. Failure is not an option. Integrity, courtesy, self-control, perseverance and indomitable spirit. These are the rules I will live my life by. I will be an example to others. I will not fail. I am looking forward to seeing my wife tomorrow. I will do my best to enjoy her company this weekend. I am very lucky to have her and probably don't deserve her. My goal will be to get back in that bedroom. No more basement.*

I had a good week. *I feel confident and content with myself. I have really learned a lot about myself this week. Journaling really helps put the day's events in order.*

The next day didn't go as smoothly. I argued with my wife. No matter how hard I tried to use my new-found coping skills, I felt worthless, guilty and had suicidal thoughts. I couldn't bring myself to sleep in the bedroom because I was hurt as a result of my wife's anger. Again I retreated to the basement.

I spent some time with my son, then prepared to return to rehab. *My daughter came home and gave me a big hug. I am sure happy she is talking to me now. She is a good kid … I love my wife with all my heart and have from the first time we met, but if things don't get better, I'm afraid we will have to go our separate ways.*

Unfortunately it's natural to feel up and down, and to take things out on the ones closest to you. At one point my wife read part of my journal and was hurt by some of the things I had written. I felt very sorry.

Back at rehab for week five, I was told again that I don't like bonding with people because I think they will leave me or die. That's why I became more solitary and cold to others and my family.

I struggled to come to terms with no longer being in SWAT. One of the group members told a story about being in the airborne. *I know he really misses it as I will miss SWAT but I have to move on. My job is not a measure of my self-worth. It has become very clear that I have no identity outside of work. It will be hard to go back to driving a patrol car. Having said that I don't know anyone who could have done or accomplished what I have in 20 years of policing. I am not a bad guy. I am a good guy who reacted with what tools were situationally appropriate for the circumstance.*

I was learning that it's a good idea to have hobbies outside of the job and friends outside of the force, and to know that you are not the job. But this is something that's difficult for officers.

Another session of EMDR and I broke down even more. *I talked about my attempted suicide. It was very unsettling. During the session I was a mess, crying and shaking uncontrollably. It was very intense. I couldn't even go for a run. I was very mixed up.*

I phoned home and spoke with my wife. I'm only starting to realize how poorly I have been treating myself since the shooting, as well as the family. I should have been in this program immediately following the shooting. I have spent the last five years setting up for a nervous breakdown. I can't believe that I couldn't see it coming. I was wrong not to listen to my wife or see how I was hurting my children. I am so sorry I put them through such an emotional roller-coaster but I didn't have the skill set to deal with the family situation and anger was the emotion I was most familiar with and could access readily.

I talked to a friend on the phone and he said I sounded good and that lots of people had been asking about me. *This made me feel better as I was having an emotional day.*

I really enjoyed writing in my journal. Who would have known what I wrote then would be coming true now? *Who knows? This may be the beginning of a new book.*

I underwent extra sessions of EMDR. People respond to different types of treatment. This was the most powerful for me. I also met with a volunteer who used to be a police officer.

I was having problems with self-nurturing, leisure time and spirituality. Then I began to have negative feelings about some of the group. *Most of the people here have no spine and are drifting through life instead of challenging it. They are weak and no matter how long they stay here they will never get better … The more I look at some of the patients here the better I feel about myself … I can't believe how self-absorbed they are.*

About midway through the program, I was able to sleep upstairs at times, go to a bar without having a drink, be out in a crowd without feeling anxious and have a conversation with my wife. Six weeks into recovery, I began to acknowledge that I was sick. *The psychologist has made it clear that I don't consider myself worthy or deserving and I must learn how to change this behaviour as it could affect my recovery … I can feel myself improving a day at a time but there is part of me that says this is bullshit; go back to work and keep your mouth shut, drive on. It is what it is and I don't deserve to get better. I don't know why I hate myself so much. This has to stop.*

In group we talked about finding the beauty in simple things. I attended a horticulture class. Afterwards I experienced a remarkable change. While the therapist was speaking, I was drawing in my workbook and sort of paying attention. I wrote on the top of the book the words "Don't fight it" and continued to draw in my book while listening to the lecture. The therapist took time to speak with me and pointed out the difference she had seen in me from my first days at rehab. She shook my hand and gave a gentle squeeze that made me feel comfortable and warm. I went downstairs and took a seat and waited for EMDR.

While I was sitting there, I finally acknowledged what people have been telling me for years. I realized that I am important. *I do count. I am kind and gentle and I have qualities that are good. I am worthwhile and deserving of self-nurturing and leisure time. I had just realized that the person Jimmy had blown through the shell I was living in for five years and I am more than my job.*

It was time for EMDR. The revelation would only be stronger. I had intense flashbacks. *I could see myself and the team at calls, and hear my teammates shouting, 'Jimmy it's over. It's over.' I broke down more than I ever had before. I felt as though I had just woken from a coma and Jimmy the gentle, kind and compassionate man was back.* It was a powerful experience.

Later I spoke to Dayle and explained what had taken place. I'm not sure she bought into the whole story but I know it happened. I listened to her problems and did not get mad as was my old way of dealing with family problems. Later I went for a walk and saw a rabbit. I was able to take the time to appreciate it for what it was.

I shared my EMDR experience with the group. It was hard but the way it occurred was so easy with the simple words, "Don't fight it." These words let me accept myself for who I am, a gentle, caring, compassionate person who has had to deal with the loss of family members and a thousand emotion-packed missions as well as trying to keep a marriage on the go and raise kids.

I tried to protect myself so much that I got lost. I shared this with the group. I noticed I was not squirming in my seat. It was like a weight being lifted off my shoulders. I explained I was worthwhile and deserving of healing. It was then I knew I would continue working with Dr. Sean P. O'Brien, a clinical psychologist who works mainly with police officers and policing organizations.

In loss group I learned that my occupation and frequency of loss had led to my emotional numbness. I had not grieved the losses of my family members, the people I encountered on the job or the team members I no longer saw daily.

The next two days were difficult but I slept upstairs both nights. Dayle was not well and had started a new job. She was under a lot of pressure. She talked about her new job and I listened. I could hear her frustration about having to handle everything herself. I understood but the longer I stayed in rehab I could see it is the way we perceive things that controls our moods.

During week seven, another group member finally spoke up, talking about how he risked his life undercover and that in return he felt his organization treated him as an outcast. *The more*

I hear this, the more angry I get. I ask what is wrong with people? Why do organizations eat their young? Why are they afraid to say our members are human? They make all kinds of efforts in the community but when it comes time to look after their own, they fail dismally. Is it any wonder we drink and take drugs and have failed marriages and suffer from depression and personality disorders? This makes me sick and saps me of any pride I once had as a police officer.

My last session of the day was EMDR. Many missions flashed before my eyes. It was very frightening. I realized that it was time to hang up my guns. *I have pushed the envelope too many times. I fear if I go back on the road I will be killed. I must be lucky every day. The bad guy only has to be lucky once.*

I had my time as a gunfighter and realized it was time to pass on my experience and knowledge to young officers. I felt a sense of relief.

At this point in my stay, I was curious yet reluctant to get the results from my psychiatric test. I hoped it confirmed PTSD as this would validate my behaviour in the past. I was nervous but welcomed the test results because it would show me what part of me needed work. With my new skill set, I had vowed to make improvements to myself. However, I knew I had to accept the results, good or bad.

The doctor changed my meds. I no longer needed a tranquilizer but received a sleeping pill. *I hate to say it but the medication is what I need to live without depression and anxious feelings.*

Many people are afraid to take medication, but it's important to get the symptoms under control. Doses may be high at first but later you will be weaned, sometimes entirely, from them.

Being a top SWAT officer had taken its toll on my family and me. I knew I could no longer be everything to everybody. I know now that all I can do is my best and that has to be enough.

Rehab was getting tiring. Some people had been there three times. As much as I felt empathy for their illness, I had to move on. This was very troubling for me as I felt cold and selfish. But I knew I must move on because the whole situation was emotionally exhausting.

As I listened to the group one after the other talking about herbal tea, incense and essential oils, I think 'get a spine.' I have had enough of this bullshit. The reality is that when I am finished here it is back to the world. Put on a happy face and go. Such is life, unfair and filled with disappointments.

I know I will fall into the routine this time without alcohol. I can only hope medication and Sean (O'Brien) will keep me from the bottle. I am determined and angry. I will use the anger to fuel my determination to stay off the drink. I know I can do it. As much as I have made breakthroughs and have come to know myself, as of today it is crystal clear that nothing has changed.

I was very frustrated with these thoughts and took every opportunity to speak with the staff and share my feelings. They were kind and concerned.

Dayle called and we talked for a while. She asked if I had been drinking during my stay. I was disappointed that she would ask me that and I felt nothing had changed.

In group we did an exercise about setting boundaries. The goal was to push bad choices away and to bring in people who would be more helpful in keeping me safe. I moved alcohol away and brought my wife and kids closer. I had no names other than my wife and the kids. I finished the exercise feeling lonely and abandoned, and in some ways hopeless. Life. You don't have to like it, you just have to do it. It was the end of week seven and I felt like a failure.

The weekend was rough. My wife and I argued. I used every grounding skill I had learned, but the argument escalated. I was tired of this and gave an ultimatum: divorce and just leave me alone or pretend everything is normal and drive on.

I don't know how many times I have said I'm going to get sick and now that I am it is a surprise to everyone. It is no surprise to me. I have spent the last 20 years putting my life on the line and that is not enough. I've taken every opportunity to work and bring home money. I worry as much about money as she does. I feel I am a failure in her eyes. Anything I have learned at rehab is useless.

Reality won't pause for me or anyone else and their feelings or emotions. It is a disappointment but the cold hard fact is my stay at rehab has only been a wait stop in my journey in life. Nobody is going to take time for me to count to 10 or take a deep breath. What is seen as a healthy lifestyle at rehab is a weakness that will be exploited. It is not about knowing my emotional self. It is all about stuffing and growing a thicker skin and being numb at all times. I don't have to like it, I just have to do it.

I never had a drink because I was feeling good. I would always start drinking when I was in a bad mood. No wonder it got out of hand. I vowed to use my new coping skills, to see Dr. O'Brien weekly and to continue to be medicated because this was the only way I could hang on. This disappointed me because I went without drinking in the past and it wasn't the drinking that was the problem, it was always something else. *This was one of the worst days I had at rehab.*

The weekend came and went and Monday morning had me feeling no better. *Each and every day for the rest of my life, I must pretend I am happy all day and cry all night.*

I was very upset over my hopeless feelings, and there was no alcohol to numb the feelings this time. The therapist was supportive and explained that these feelings are part of the process and said I was using skill sets. I appreciated her concern however; I felt hopeless.

I noticed that I was having tremors and my hands were shaking, making it hard for me to pick up a coffee without spilling it. I was a nervous wreck.

Throughout my ordeal there were a few friends (former colleagues) who stood by me. I phoned one and had a long talk. He was very supportive of me and has always been at my side. He understands how much output of emotions there has been over the years. He said I do well at anything I do and deep down I knew this was true.

I felt like shit but I wouldn't give in. I knew the fight wasn't over. I decided I would no longer worry about what other people think. The long talk with my colleague did a lot of good.

I was and am a person suffering from an illness and it is treatable. I will get better as each day passes. I grow stronger. Before my wife can respect me I must respect myself.

I started to notice my memory was getting bad. *I don't know where the last two years went. I only notice the lapse in time when I watch the news or read a paper about a current or what I think is a current event (but it) happened a year ago.*

I tried to watch TV with the group, but I could taste the medication and my mouth was dry. I had difficulty preventing intrusive thoughts from breaking my concentration. The thoughts jumped from recent events to the past, things from childhood to police things.

The next day I shared my thoughts of the last week with the group and was surprised at the response. It didn't bring them down. They were helpful as always.

The doctor prepared us for release and also explained the history of PTSD and the reluctance of some agencies to accept this diagnosis.

I also thought about graduation. What would I say? I would miss the group but I looked forward to my second chance. Some group members were afraid. We offered each other support.

I was given a return to work letter. My assessment confirmed what I already knew – I have PTSD. It would be more fuel to the fire to help my return to work. *I am prepared for anything they throw at me. Nothing they say or do will be as bad as my last five years. I control my life.*

It was a quiet weekend. I ordered pizza with my son and slept lightly because I had to go pick up my daughter from a friend's. I slept upstairs with my wife.

On Sunday Dayle and I went for a walk and stopped for hamburgers. As we walked toward Harvey's, she held my hand. This small gesture made me feel worthwhile and loved. It is the small things that are the glue of the relationship.

It was time to go back to rehab. I was bittersweet about the last days of treatment. I would miss the group.

The group was anxious as we neared the end. However, I was more aware of my feelings and potential than I had ever been. I felt strong, positive and ready for life's Round 2.

I am ready to land, punch and knock out. I will still need coaching. The difference is this time I will listen.

I had an appointment regarding my progress during the course. It was measured on a graduated scale. The same questions were asked at the beginning and the end of the course. My highest scores at the start were one or two and by the end of the program they were eight or nine. It was a major accomplishment.

The graduation ceremony was very difficult. The bond and trust that the group formed was strong. Everyone took turns talking and diplomas were given out. I was described as a gentle giant, strong and courageous but warm and tender. I was deeply touched by the statement.

When I stood up to say thank you to the group, I was calm, with no butterflies or apprehension. I was comfortable because the group had accepted me. If I had made a mistake or stumbled, there would have been no judgment, just support. At the conclusion I thanked the group and received warm applause. Many people offered words of encouragement.

I remember feeling that I would be a crusader for PTSD. *I have an image of me on a book cover or teaming with Dr. O'Brien or starting a support group. I hear a calling.*

The morning came too fast. *The custom is to take a small rock as a reminder of the safety home represents. It is my turn. I bring in a large rock as a symbol of my burden and abuse. The group laughs. I recover quickly. The large rock represents large problems I could not manage. I trade it in for a very small rock.*

Next was the hard part – the goodbyes. There wasn't a dry eye in the ward. I was taken aback by the outpouring of love and encouragement. People kept coming up and thanking me and saying things like you are the father I never had. I had a profound effect on the group and it was hard for me to believe.

I got into the truck and headed downtown. There was one more thing left to do.

3

*"Our job is such that we can follow each and
every procedure to the letter and yet a person dies."*

Closure

I had one last thing to do before this part of my journey ended.
It was to walk into St. Michael's Hospital and rescue Jimmy.
I had planned to visit St. Mike's for a long time, but was anxious
and apprehensive about actually going back.

On the last day of rehab, a cold day in March 2005, I
gave one of my fellow trauma survivors a ride to the airport on
my way back to Toronto, perhaps hoping it would give me time
to talk myself out of continuing on to the hospital. If there wasn't
enough time, I could do it another day, I reasoned. But I dropped
my friend at the airport, said good luck and headed downtown.

As I drove to Toronto I was shaking and nervous. It got
more difficult to concentrate. It was late afternoon. I parked on
Church Street and walked to the hospital, entering off Queen

Street. The smell of the hospital swept over me as I walked down the halls. I wondered what I would say if someone was to ask where I was going, or what I was doing. My heart raced as I approached the emergency department. Tears welled up in my eyes and I could hear a former teammate saying, "It's over. It is time to go home."

The emergency room had changed since 2000. It had been renovated but I was able to find the spot where Henry Masuka, with his baby nearby, held the doctor hostage. I could feel the pressure increasing.

As I sat down at what was then the nurses' station, the night of that New Year's Eve played out each moment, step by step. I realized I could change nothing that had happened. What I could change were my feelings toward the events that had taken place. Blame and fault are words that imply intent, but there was no intent in any of my actions. I was doing the job to the best of my ability. Police officers are good people who find themselves caught up in situations because that is the nature of their work. I wished there had been a better outcome. Our job is such that we can follow each and every procedure to the letter and yet a person dies.

At the end of the day, no apology is required for the team's actions because there was no intent on our part, only hope that our action resolved the matter at hand. In this case we had successfully rescued the hostage.

I sat for about five minutes, gathered my thoughts and walked out the rear door. I walked back to the truck and drove home. My eyes were full of tears. I thought, "Now I know it's over. Jimmy has come home. A job well done. The mission took five years but now the mission is complete. I have brought everyone home safely."

It was closure for this chapter in my life, and as happy an ending as it seemed, the journey was far from over. In the years to come my struggle would continue, but the weight has gotten lighter with therapy and time.

There will be good days and bad days ahead but there are certainly a lot fewer bad days now that I understand PTSD and myself better.

For a long time after St. Mike's, I had trouble setting foot in a hospital. Now, through the journey, I have learned to live for the now and not for the what was, or the what will be. This is how I keep moving forward.

The key to staying on track is unconditional acceptance and forgiveness, and no expectations. It may sound simplistic, but try it, you might be surprised at the outcome.

4

"Remember, even the longest journey begins with the first step. Having said that, you must know that your recovery will continue for the rest of your life."

A New Chapter Begins

I spent two months in rehab and emerged with skill sets, medication and a therapist. I had been diagnosed with PTSD and was determined to get better. I told clinical psychologist Dr. Sean P. O'Brien, "I'm going to be the best patient you ever had."

I discovered the biggest obstacle that stands between law enforcement officers and recovery is ourselves. We spend time maintaining control of crime scenes, hoping that control will give us the power we need to survive. Unfortunately this maladaptive control freak behaviour carries over into our personal lives.

When we enter a room, we immediately look for the rear exit. We do a quick scan of the people on the premises and when we sit down our back is to the wall and every person who comes through the door is subject to close scrutiny. If you have been on the job for a while, you have heard your significant other say, "You're not a cop at home." But how do you turn the need for control on and off?

I had to learn to relinquish control of my recovery to the professionals. This was the most difficult part. I had to remember that asking for help did not make me weak.

I also had to understand that recovery wouldn't happen overnight. It's common for patients to try to calculate how many weeks they are going to be in a rehab program and to try to book the next available shift to go back to work – fully cured, of course. I was no different when I entered rehab but soon realized it would be necessary to practice my personal skills with the same enthusiasm and vigour that I practiced my tactical skills. Remember, even the longest journey begins with the first step. That said you must know that your recovery will continue for the rest of your life.

2004-2005

When I left rehab, there is no question it was a struggle. I went through a stage where I wondered if all of the effort was worth it and I thought it might be best to give up.

I still had a lot of issues to deal with, including an impaired driving charge, and they weighed heavy on my heart.

I continued to see Sean, sometimes two times a day, three or four times a week. His office became my safe place. I was like a lion in the circus that sits on a stool where he is safe and not subject to the whip.

At some point between the tears, I asked if Sean would

be interested in providing lectures on the subject of Critical Incident Stress. Sean was very supportive and almost immediately we started to put together a lecture about Post Traumatic Stress Disorder. It gave me something to focus on.

Sean sees our work as part of my treatment as I continue to gather self-confidence. The more I am exposed to my experiences in a safe environment, the less painful and more removed the memories become. I also wanted then, and now, to help fellow officers avoid what I have gone through.

As well as seeing Sean, I went to AA meetings at night, but I found it a little difficult, almost overwhelming. I was still pretty raw emotionally. I will say this: there is something about receiving the coins that track your progress. It lifts your spirits and gives you a feeling of accomplishment.

I had stopped drinking. I'm not sure how it happened. I have not had a drink since. I firmly believe I was not an alcoholic. I also attended a support group for two hours each week. It was a little easier than AA because it was exclusive to police officers. However, it had quite a negative edge to it. The group seemed to focus more on how the job is screwed up and on bullshit than on getting well.

There is something else I would like to point out. With the exception of sessions with Sean, at every group I attended, I had to start every meeting with, "My name is Jim and I am an alcoholic." This upset me.

There is no question I had developed a dependence on alcohol, but I didn't need the extra guilt associated with admitting to alcoholism, which I felt was an incorrect statement. I felt the true issue was the PTSD. In fact as I started to attend the weekly group session more regularly, I would begin with, "My name is Jim and I am a trauma survivor." It was much easier.

A Chance to Move On

One of my bosses told me about an opening at the new gun-gang unit in the firearms section. I said yes right away and requested a transfer. The transfer went through and there I was in front of a new boss. Immediately I tried to point out that there was more to my circumstance than drinking, and tried to assure him I would not let him down.

I was quite surprised at his response. "I know you won't let me down. I know all about you and obviously something went wrong somewhere," he told me. It was refreshing. He is an outstanding senior officer and human being.

I diligently continued my treatment – appointments with doctors and psychologists and group work and medication.

Home life was still quite rough. My wife still had a lot of understandable anger over the whole situation. I felt terrible and still do on some days, but we can only change what we have control over. It is part of letting go.

There were a number of court dates for the impaired driving charge and there was a great deal of stress involved each time. I was worried I would lose my job – not so much the job but my livelihood. It would have been hard on the entire family.

In June 2005 I attended my trial for impaired. I was well supported by members of my new unit and some close friends.

I met with the arresting officer and apologized for my behaviour. I probably should have thanked him, but I was not far enough along in my recovery to think of it. The officer took the stand and gave his evidence in a professional, efficient manner.

Now it was my turn. I took the stand and told the story. It was difficult and I felt like crying but just managed to hold back the tears.

Then it was time for the judge to speak his piece and though he had empathy for my situation, I was convicted of the impaired driving charge and went a year without a licence.

This was not good but was what I had expected. It was difficult, but I phoned my wife to tell her. The bad news only intensified the tension at home. And now I was on foot and would be taking public transit or depending on my wife to get me to where I had to be. It was humiliating.

It was difficult not being able to do simple things like pick up my kids after school. Meeting them at the bus stop just wasn't doing it, but I struggled on. What else could I do?

I did a lot of walking that year but with each step I thought about my situation. Walking can be lonely when you have troubled thoughts. It was on one of these lonely walks that I realized how lucky I was to have my wife and her support.

I didn't have trouble accepting responsibility for my actions and if a suspended licence and impaired conviction was the result of my actions, I accepted it. I would later be acquitted of the impaired charge.

Through all the bad, it was hard to remember that my experiences with the police service weren't all negative. Some bosses thought the SWAT team and I did a good job. For a long time, I was happy on the job.

5

*"My boss took the stand as my character witness.
He called me a poster child for recovery."*

The Unexpected

2005-2006

As time went by, my wife, Dayle, and I had periods where we
could talk without arguing or reliving the past. In one of
these quiet moments, I told her I wanted to provide lectures about
PTSD and my experiences.

My wife in her wisdom and with the faith she had in me
that I had lost, suggested we form a company, Bremner Associates
Inc. I would say, "Who would call?" I still lacked self-confidence.

My wife enrolled in a small business course and developed
a business plan. We built a website and sent out flyers to police
agencies across Canada. Dr. O'Brien and I were booked for one
lecture, which lead to another and another. We were getting good
reviews. We were on the right track. It was good to see some police

services wanted to get the topic of PTSD out in the open.

The requests were a great boost to my self-esteem, but I thought that in some small way the requests were charitable. I still had a great deal of self-doubt.

But the phone did not stop ringing. I was amazed and humbled by it. I still have trouble believing police agencies would ask me to talk to their most skilled tactical officers.

I also found myself being approached by officers who wanted to know if I thought they were drinking too much or who had questions about PTSD. Others shared their experiences with me. I was happy to provide support. All they wanted was unconditional acceptance and a non-judgmental listener, and I could provide that. I also continued my own treatment with Sean as well as my group work.

2006-2007

Almost a year to the day of my impaired driving conviction, the phone at my desk rang. I picked it up and heard a voice say, "You have been acquitted." I thought it was a joke because I forgot about the appeal and did not expect a reversal in the matter. I hung the phone back up and continued my work. About 20 minutes later my phone rang again and it was my inspector. He informed me that I had been acquitted and the message started to sink in. Even though I was acquitted of the impaired charge, I still carry a lot of guilt and shame over the whole incident. I was also still facing Police Act charges for discreditable conduct.

Sean and I continued to speak at large events and were

getting great feedback. It seemed that our mission was having an effect. Officers, their superiors, psychologists and psychiatrists were becoming more aware of PTSD and what to do about it, now seeing it as a normal response to an abnormal situation.

After the talks, psychologists and psychiatrists came up to us and told us what we had said was hitting home. Officers thanked us. For officers, articulating our feelings can be difficult but it's amazing what happens when we're given permission to acknowledge those feelings.

I did have a bit of a setback in 2007 that still bothers me. After a speaking engagement I received a phone call from an old teammate. He felt I had suggested that he was dealing with PTSD. What I said was that no one is untouched by Critical Incident Stress but it caused a falling out and we rarely speak now and that hurts. It was clear that my open views on PTSD were not popular with everyone. It only made me more determined to continue the mission.

2008-2009

Almost a year to the day of my acquittal of the impaired charge, it was time to face my Police Services Act charges for the same incident. I found this a difficult time. The same system that was interested in what I was saying about PTSD would pursue a conviction under the Police Act for discreditable conduct.

I attended the hearing and listened as the prosecutor who had empathy for my situation read in the charges.

I was feeling better after rehab and regular appointments

with Dr. O'Brien, but it was difficult to take the additional stress of these charges. The only good thing about the experience was that my boss took the stand as my character witness. He called me a poster child for recovery. He was outstanding. It really helped my self-worth.

However I was found guilty of the Police Act charges and had to work 17 days without pay. I worked those days straight away. I thought it best to get it all behind me and start my new history.

Television Police Drama *Flashpoint*

Flashpoint is something I never saw coming. I received a phone call from an old SWAT colleague, S/Sgt. Barney McNeilly. Barney is a retired veteran with over 35 years with the police service, the last 16 with SWAT. It is important to mention Barney as he has always been at my side and was responsible for selecting me for the tactical team. He did my entrance exam. Barney asked me to share my views on PTSD with two writers for a police drama pilot episode that would follow an urban tactical team through their lives and calls.

I reluctantly called and set up a meeting with Mark Ellis and Stephanie Morgenstern, the show's creators and writers. I don't know what they expected but I think they were surprised. I told them everything, some of it almost moving me to tears. I held back, but I think they saw through me. I bared my soul in a way that was cathartic. Much to my surprise they seemed fascinated and supportive at the same time. The writers would email me scripts and call me with technical questions regarding weapons and equipment.

Once again I was surprised when executive producers Bill Mustos and Anne Marie La Traverse brought me on as the tactical police consultant. I was assisting the actors with their tactical skills. I was training a team again. I considered the cast my team.

Everyone was great and always took the time to thank me for my help. As much as I shared with the *Flashpoint* writers and cast about how helpful being part of the production was for me, and how much it meant to me to be part of *Flashpoint*, I don't think they fully appreciated how much it meant to me. After all, it was only a few years before that suicide looked like the best option. It was great to be able to use my skills again and to be appreciated and respected.

With each new episode, I grew more confident. *Flashpoint* gave me a sense of self and my potential beyond policing.

Meeting and working with *Flashpoint* star Hugh Dillon, who portrays sniper Ed Lane, was most uplifting as we both spent time in rehab. We had an immediate respect and empathy for each other. He gets it and knows what I'm talking about when I talk about my worst days.

2009 and Beyond

All the while I have continued to share my PTSD experiences with officers across the country. In 2009 I began working on the book I first thought about in rehab. At times it's been cathartic, other times it's been draining to recall the events. But I need you to see that the bad passes and you'll be left with the good. I am void, for the most part, of bad feelings about the whole thing. I think it is the detachment from the events that allows me to move forward in a positive way. I'm determined. The message must get out. The cop mentality of being afraid to ask for help must be broken!

6

"Police officers are the only people who get to meet society's worst one per cent, one hundred per cent of the time. Our negative attitude is reinforced each time we answer a call for service. Break the cycle."

Knowledge Is Power

When I speak with officers struggling with PTSD and they ask me about a treatment program, I am not surprised to hear them say, "So the program is eight weeks long and when I complete it I'll be better, right?" Wrong! It's important to note that these programs give the PTSD victim a set of guidelines and tools that must be put into practice after the treatment program comes to an end.

Make no mistake. Recovery is an ongoing process. Every day you must fight for your life. That may sound extreme, but the statistics about suicide and law enforcement officers are grim. The U.S. Bureau of Labor reports that police have a seven times greater risk of dying from suicide than the average worker. Police are safer at work than they are when they're off duty, when most suicides happen.

If not for your physical well-being, you will be fighting to regain the quality of your life; but remember, the work gets easier as time passes. Knowing what to expect and how to help yourself is key.

Psychological Treatment

I spent time with my psychologist Dr. O'Brien at first twice a day, three or four days a week. As time passed, I saw him three days a week, then two, then one. After one year I saw him twice a month, then reduced my visits to once a month. Now, I see him as required to help clear my mind of garbage.

Many of us, because of stigma, are concerned about seeing a psychologist, but try to look at it like this. Treat your visit to the psychologist as if you are going to the dentist. We don't question going to the dentist every six months as a preventive measure. Try to look at your visit to a psychologist the same way.

PTSD has been in the news more and more as soldiers return from combat and display numerous symptoms. For soldiers, insurgents are an issue because with the enemy disguised as citizens, it's no longer clear who the enemy is. What we need to remember is that's what it's like for cops every day – every person is a potential threat. Cops are exposed to urban warfare for 20 years or more. It's no wonder PTSD is a problem for us. Get help.

Medication

Let's talk medication. Again the stigma issue crops up, so think of your medication like this. If you were a diabetic, you would not question your daily dose of insulin – you have a physiological need for a chemical your body is no longer able to produce.

Consult your doctor regarding your medication because it may need to be adjusted from time to time. Remember, as time passes you will require less and eventually may be able to wean yourself from it.

I always find it frustrating when officers resist medication but think nothing of drinking a 26er of Scotch. Isn't that medication? I travelled that road myself until I changed my perspective about prescription medication and its benefits.

I can only emphasize the importance of medication. The role it has played in getting me back on my feet is this: if a doctor told me taking medication for PTSD symptoms would take five years off my life, I would gladly accept it so I would never return to the turmoil and chaos of my life with PTSD and without medication.

Support Groups

It is important to continue group work after leaving a treatment facility because you will require a non-judgmental, unconditionally accepting support group that can give you honest feedback and guidance on your recovery.

If you don't have a support group in your area, start one. This may sound like a daunting task, but it is really quite simple. It doesn't require any funding, official sanction or record keeping, and that's the beauty of it. I run my support group out of a coffee shop across from my office. I see fellow officers at various points in their recovery and we just talk – well, they talk and I listen. It is important to be a good listener.

Self-Care

We can start with some very basic items like improving our self-care – good body hygiene and grooming. Start a fitness program, join the YMCA or simply take time in the day to go for a walk. It might help to keep a daily log of your activities.

Eat properly and get your rest. You need eight hours of restful sleep and if you need medication to get it, don't be afraid to ask your doctor.

Take part in activities that help your recovery. Support can be found where you least expect it. Take a chance. Speak to a person you may not have spoken to in the past because they aren't in law enforcement. You might be surprised to find that people outside police circles are quite empathetic about the effects of PTSD. You may have to force yourself at first, but make yourself do it. Remaining sociable is important.

Nurturing

It has been my experience that people suffering from PTSD, myself included, are not the type of people who spend much time looking after themselves. Nurturing and self-reward for a job well done are foreign concepts for us. However, all is not lost. It is really a simple task. All you have to do is take the time to treat yourself to a speciality coffee, read a book or go for a walk; it is time for yourself. You will be working hard on recovery and you deserve some reward for your efforts.

New History

What a unique opportunity PTSD has given you, something that other people don't get: a chance to start a new life, a new history.

Our struggle with PTSD and its effects and our attempt to self-medicate have given the people around us a skewed view of our personality and behaviour, so let's change that.

It has been my experience that people spend a lot of time worrying about what the world thinks of us. But the world is a big place and we are not that significant.

If I were to ask you how many people you came into contact with today and what you recall about your meeting, or what you know about their background and personal life, you would be challenged to give me an answer. Guess what? You're one of those people to someone else.

So let's take advantage of people and their short-term memories by creating a new history. It's about replacing old bad habits with good ones. We must break free of bad behaviour to create a new history. Don't give people an opportunity to assume you have not changed because you continue to frequent your old haunts. Your spouse will have a hard time believing you went out with the guys to the local pub and you didn't have a drink.

This is not a trust issue and it's not about you; don't forget about the vicarious trauma your family has suffered as a result of the PTSD and your alcohol or drug abuse. Your spouse's disbelief in you is based on your old history and entrenched in the fear that things haven't changed.

(See Chapter 9, *A Note from Home*, for an idea of what your family may be going through.)

In a very short period of time people will only remember your new history of good behaviour. The positive reinforcement received from their acceptance and support will do wonders to bolster your self-esteem and take you out of a negative psychological posture.

Bad Habits

Probably the most important part of creating a new history is to lose the old behaviours that dragged us to the bottom. This is a difficult challenge because there are no doubt peers involved. Close to everyone who struggles with an addiction of any type, you will find an enabler. This person makes it easy for you to keep or return to your bad habits. If the guys can't meet you anywhere except at the local watering hole or can't do without a drink after any activity, you are in grave danger of returning to the old routine.

I am not saying you can't ever return to that group of people, but in recovery you are in a delicate state and can be easily influenced by negative attitudes on a day when you may be struggling emotionally. That makes returning to drinking too easy. You have to figure out how to stay away from bad influences and not get dragged back into negative behaviour.

Friends

If one thing is true, it's that an experience like PTSD has a way of making it clear who the special people in your life truly are. Those people are the ones who have the fortitude to tell you the truth about your behaviour.

The people who tolerate your bad behaviour are easier to hang out with and the enabler in the crowd tells you only what you want to hear, which only perpetuates the problem. Breaking free of the people who are not helping you move forward is the most important thing you can do.

By starting new activities and hobbies, or just getting back to an activity you enjoy, you will start to develop new relationships with people who are more conducive to your recovery. You may have to force yourself at first, but do it.

It is interesting to meet people who live outside the police culture and find out about their points of view. You will be surprised to find out you have similar interests, human interests. "Hey I'm like everyone else!" What a relief!

Negativity

Police culture is fraught with negative attitudes because of the skewed view of society we develop as a result of dealing with trauma on a daily basis. Police officers are the only people who get to meet society's worst one per cent, one hundred per cent of the time. Our negative attitude is reinforced each time we answer a call for service. Break the cycle.

You must make an effort to connect with people who are not in the service – friends you may not have seen for years because your whole world for a long time now has been nothing but other cops.

I will no longer tolerate negative thoughts in my daily life or allow myself to be dragged down that road. As much as I like the gang I work with, I can't attend the morning bull session because it is the same conversation every day – how the job is screwed and everything is bullshit. I'm sure you've heard it. Why start the day with this mantra?

Use positive affirmations, read materials and books about people who have overcome adversity. It can't help but motivate you in a positive manner.

Avoid a Victim Mentality

Don't be a victim; taking up the role of the victim only hinders your recovery and makes your recovery dependent on other people – people you have no control over. Take ownership of your condition and start healing and continue to heal.

Have you noticed the other groups of people who suffer from medical conditions and who are featured in the media? They take proud ownership of their afflictions. Probably the most inspirational are the disabled. They take part in directing the type and quality of care and are involved in athletics and intellectual endeavours. Post Traumatic Stress Disorder must be met with the same enthusiasm.

Never Give Up

Indomitable spirit is one of the five tenets of tae kwon do. For years I practiced this martial art and held this belief but never had an opportunity to put it into practice.

It means sticking with your new history and the way you have chosen to live your new life no matter what. There is no question that there will be days when you will struggle, but take it minute by minute, hour by hour, day by day.

Every minute you practice your new history is a minute farther from the life you used to live. It will make you stronger, boost your morale and strengthen your indomitable spirit. Soon you will be unbreakable.

Remember, though, it's important to keep the door open for future treatment. Before you become overwhelmed by stress, see your doctor or talk to your group for support.

7

"I soon realized it would be necessary to practice
my personal skills with the same enthusiasm
and vigour as I practice my tactical skills."

How to Avoid PTSD

Most police officers are familiar with the 10 fatal errors of policing. Along with those errors, which can result in physical harm, I have added errors to be aware of in order to avoid mental harm.

1. ATTITUDE: If you fail to keep your mind on the job or you carry personal problems into the field, you will make errors. It can cost you or your fellow officers their lives.

The nature of police work has a way of transforming our positive attitude into one of pessimism and negativity. The situations we are injected into are a great strain on our emotions and yes, our feelings get hurt.

Our body looks after us by developing defence mechanisms

such as anger, aggression, shutting down and non-involvement, which can carry over to home.

Non-involvement means you no longer make time for activities you used to enjoy. You withdraw from people. "I don't want to go to your sister's birthday." "I would rather stay home tonight." "Do we have to go out for dinner?"

Most men will retreat to the basement or garage and detach themselves from their loved ones because it is less painful than sharing the events of the day. We want to protect our families from the violence we witness daily.

2. TOMBSTONE COURAGE: *No one doubts that you have courage, but in any situation where time allows, wait for backup. There are few instances where you should try to make a dangerous apprehension unaided.*

Understand that you will need plenty of backup on this one. You are neither trained nor equipped to deal with PTSD. Let the medical and psychological professionals help you. Friends and colleagues can offer support, but don't let them carry you.

If your friends are your drinking buddies, prepare to relapse. Develop realistic boundaries you can keep until you are farther along in your recovery. Meet them for coffee instead of at the local watering hole.

Once I asked, I was astonished at how many people wanted to help, some of whom I least expected. Some people you might want to talk to are a minister, a psychologist, a psychiatrist, a family doctor, a fellow officer who has been through it or a support group. You will feel better just by talking to someone.

3. NOT ENOUGH REST: *To do your job you must be alert. Being sleepy or asleep on the job is not only against regulations, but can endanger you, the community and your fellow officers.*

Rest. What can I tell you about rest that you don't already know? You don't get enough. To bring our mind and body back into a normal range of operation, we police officers need between eight and 12 hours of sleep.

You and your spouse must ensure that you get enough rest. It is as important as eating. Catnapping is not enough. Proper rest means eight hours of restful sleep. You may have to take medication because as the symptoms of PTSD increase, your ability to have restful sleep decreases. Don't be afraid to talk to your doctor, and don't be afraid to take the medication prescribed. It can make all the difference in helping you get back on track.

I suffered from night terrors. I would fall asleep and then spend most of the night sleepwalking and carrying on conversations. When I got up the next day I would wonder why I was so tired.

4. TAKING A BAD POSITION: *Never let anyone you are questioning or detaining manipulate you into a position of disadvantage. Always be aware of position. Maintain the advantage. There is no such thing as a routine arrest or stop. Taking a bad position, like a bad attitude, creeps up on us slowly and unknowingly.*

As our body develops an emotional defence mechanism, we find ourselves withdrawing from what used to be our normal range of values. We think we're OK, it is the world that is messed up."

Tactically I have never taken a position from which I can't retreat. As we withdraw from our social network and activities, we find we are digging ourselves into a hole that is very difficult to get out of. Simply, there is no line of retreat. You will soon find that you run out of ammunition and supplies – your support network. Based on my tactical experience, these scenarios end in only one of two ways: surrender or suicide.

5. DANGER SIGNS: *As an officer you should recognize danger signs. Fast movement and strange cars are warnings that should alert you to watch and approach with caution. Know your community and watch for what looks out of place.*

Don't ignore the danger signs. The people closest to you will let you know that you are exhibiting the danger signs – drinking, spending time alone and not participating in important family activities. Your well-entrenched bad position has altered your self-awareness and you suffer from a lack of clarity, so listen to others.

6. FAILURE TO WATCH THE HANDS OF A SUSPECT: *Is he reaching for a weapon or getting ready to strike you? How else can a potential killer strike but with his hands?*

Failure to watch your hands or more importantly what is in them – drink, drugs, food or cards – is a mistake. I learned early in my career that it is the hands that kill and they ultimately carry out the last action of the suicidal officer. Who are we now shaking hands with? Will they help our recovery or will they hinder it? Be aware of who you spend time with.

If you have no one to shake hands with, you have totally

withdrawn. That's a danger sign. If you find your hands clenched, this is an indicator of stress. The closed hand does damage. The open hand is inviting.

7. RELAXING TOO SOON: *Observe carefully. Are you certain the crisis is over? Don't be quick to relax simply because the immediate and apparent threat has been neutralized.*

Often when officers join a support group, I ask what they expect from recovery. They tell me that they want to enter a program and at the end of it be good to go.

From the outset of recovery you must play an active role and your participation must be constant and ongoing. People make the mistake of thinking that if they have not had a drink in weeks they can go to the platoon party and be OK. *Wrong!*

This is relaxing too soon. You must maintain your emotional vigilance in order to stay on track. Support groups will help you stay in check and keep you within your recovery boundaries.

8. IMPROPER USE, OR NO USE, OF HANDCUFFS: *See that the hand that can kill is safely cuffed. Once you have made an arrest, handcuff the prisoner immediately and properly.*

Just as you secure and cuff the living wounded and dead to maintain your physical safety, you must also handcuff the adversaries of your emotional safety – drinks, drugs, food or gambling. Cuffing, or boundary-setting, means you may have to find other ways to interact with your colleagues. Movies, a coffee and other safe activities are what you need. Never loosen the cuffs. If you do, I guarantee you will get hurt.

9. NO SEARCH OR POOR SEARCH: *There are so many places to hide weapons that your failure to search is a crime against you and your fellow officers. Many criminals carry several weapons and are prepared to use them against you.*

No search or poor search of the soul will doom you to relapse. You must take time with the help of trained professionals to find what it is that is ailing you. It has taken you some time to get sick and the issues are well rooted. It will take you a while to dig out.

This is an opportunity to discover what makes you tick and get back to normal. I warn you though, searching your soul can be painful.

10. DIRTY OR INOPERABLE WEAPON: *Are your weapons clean? Will they fire? What's the sense of carrying any firearm that may not work when you need it the most? What about the ammunition? When did you last fire so that you can hit a target in combat conditions?*

As a tactical officer I am often asked, "What is your best weapon?" My reply is, "My mind." We have learned how to clean and inspect our weaponry and we must learn to take the same care with our minds.

A regular cleaning and maintenance of the mind, with time for reflection and removal of unneeded thoughts or concerns, and with a proper debriefing are essential. Group work with trained professionals is also imperative.

The lesson behind the 10 fatal errors leading to PTSD is to be aware, to think and to wear your body and emotional armor.

I soon realized it is necessary to practice my personal skills with the same enthusiasm and vigour as I practice my tactical skills. You need to learn to do the same.

8

The Doctor Says
By Dr. Sean P. O'Brien

Author's note: Dr. Sean P. O'Brien has been an important part of my recovery. Sean is a registered clinical psychologist who has a private practice in the Toronto area. In my opinion, he is the foremost authority in the treatment of PTSD in Canada. The majority of his work involves providing clinical services to police officers and policing organizations throughout the Greater Toronto Area. He has more than 15 years of experience in dealing with high-profile critical incidents including police-related shootings, traumatic homicides, suicides and criminal investigations into police conduct.

Sean, who sees our lectures as part of my recovery, has been at my side at speaking engagements providing clinical background on PTSD. We work together to demystify Post Traumatic Stress Disorder and offer strategies officers can use to reduce their risk of developing PTSD.

Training exercises such as rapid deployment tactics have helped officers respond safely and effectively to dangerous situations. However, while tactical trainers have helped officers develop the skills necessary to deal with violent confrontations, many have fallen short when it comes to training officers how to cope with the emotional and physical problems that often follow a violent incident.

The very nature of police work puts officers in harm's way, not only physically but emotionally. Officers are continually exposed to traumatic events such as physical assaults and homicides. A high level of physiological and psychological stress in response to urban combat is normal, but if you aren't prepared to deal with your reactions appropriately, PTSD and related problems such as alcohol abuse, depression, panic attacks and suicide can result.

So unlike other tactical training scenarios, effective stress management exercises for the police need to begin, rather than end, when shots are fired. Officers must be taught to handle traumatic mental stress experiences as effectively, and as automatically, as they would handle a gun-toting bandit.

What Is Post Traumatic Stress Disorder?

The more an officer is exposed to traumatic events, the more likely it is that he or she will develop Post Traumatic Stress Disorder, a severe set of symptoms that can develop following a critical incident.

You need to know that having disturbing feelings about an incident is normal and that it's OK to talk about them. Drowning them with alcohol or hiding or ignoring your emotions is not the answer.

Diagnosing PTSD

In many cases, officers may go untreated for lengthy periods of time because the symptoms of PTSD are not widely recognized. However, diagnosing PTSD is important because if detected early, it can be treated with relatively brief forms of intervention (Fairbank, Ebert and Caddell, 2001; Foa and Rothbaum, 1998). If not, it may take years to remedy. In some cases of severe untreated trauma, the problem may never completely resolve.

Being under constant stress and remaining in a state of hypervigilance (an enhanced state of sensory sensitivity accompanied by exaggerated behaviours to detect threats) can alter the chemistry and structure of the brain and those changes are difficult to reverse if treatment does not commence in a timely manner.

According to the Diagnostic and Statistical Manual of Mental Disorders (DSM-IV-TR; American Psychiatric Association, 2000), a diagnostic manual for stress reactions, in order for a diagnosis of PTSD to be made, the officer must first have exposure to a traumatic event that involved actual or threatened death or serious injury. The officer's response to this event must involve intense fear, helplessness or horror.

Next we see the development of symptoms that come together in three clusters. You can use the following three lists as an indication of whether you or someone you know may have Post Traumatic Stress Disorder.

The traumatic event tends to be re-experienced in one or more of the following ways:

1. Intrusive and distressing recollections of the event.

2. Recurrent distressing dreams of the event.

3. Acting or feeling as if the traumatic event is recurring (for example, illusions, hallucinations, dissociative flashbacks).

4. Intense psychological distress when exposed to situations that resemble the traumatic event.

5. Physical reactions when exposed to situations that resemble the traumatic event.

Next there are three or more symptoms that represent an officer avoiding situations that are associated with the traumatic event. These symptoms include:

1. Efforts to avoid thoughts, feelings or conversations associated with the trauma.

2. Efforts to avoid activities, places or people that arouse recollections of the trauma.

3. An inability to recall an important aspect of the trauma.

4. Markedly diminished interest or participation in significant activities.

5. Feeling detached or estranged from others.

6. A restricted range of emotions, for example, inability to have loving feelings.

7. A sense of a foreshortened future, for example, the person does not expect to have a career, marriage, children or a normal life span.

Finally, there are two or more symptoms of increased arousal:

1. Difficulty falling or staying asleep.

2. Irritability or outbursts of anger.

3. Difficulty concentrating.

4. Hypervigilance, an enhanced state of sensory sensitivity accompanied by exaggerated behaviours to detect threats. It contributes to exhaustion and burnout.

5. Exaggerated startle response.

If the symptoms last for more than one month, and if they cause significant distress or impairment, PTSD is the likely diagnosis.

The Risk of Developing PTSD

Officers are continually exposed to severe forms of physical and emotional trauma, urban combat and/or have also been threatened or assaulted with a weapon. The more they are exposed to traumatic events, the more likely they are to develop a PTSD.

You're Not Alone

Some experts suggest that up to one-third of on-duty and retired police officers struggle with unresolved emotional issues associated with traumatic and violent events they encounter while on the job (Lewis, 2004). Unfortunately, most don't address these issues in a meaningful way and this can be disastrous. Untreated, PTSD can fuel many problems, including police suicide. Statistics suggest that for every officer who is killed in the line of duty, three are lost to suicide (Turvey, 1995). It has been estimated that we lose one officer to suicide across North America about every 24 hours (Lewis, 2004).

Not a Weakness

Despite these alarming statistics, most officers are reluctant to seek help because they don't want to appear to be weak and don't want to be stigmatized. Yet the reality is that stress experiences are common following a critical incident. Failing to address them in an open and direct manner is no different than an officer rejecting medical help because he feels that, "Real men don't need surgery."

Dynamics of Combat

What many officers describe as strange or unusual responses to a traumatic event are not really strange or unexpected at all. They are normal and adaptive responses that help our bodies and minds cope with trauma. However, an officer needs to be prepared for these responses, so that when he or she experiences them, it will not be overwhelming.

Physiological Effects of Urban Combat

As the seminal work by D. Grossman and his colleagues has demonstrated, at rest the normal heart rate is in the 60 to 80 beats per minute range, but during a critical incident, an officer's heart rate can accelerate to over 200 beats per minute (Grossman, 2008; Laur, 2002). This acceleration of heart rate is accompanied by a number of hormonal changes in the body.

First, the heart rate increases because the brain sets off an alarm response. The brain sends a signal that activates the sympathetic nervous system, the part of the body that is charged with keeping us alive during threatening situations. What occurs when this system is activated is an epinephrine and norepinephrine dump from the adrenal glands. Our brain also sends a signal to the heart to speed up and to increase the force of each heart contraction.

Heart Races, Breathing Becomes Rapid

Once the heart rate hits about 115 bpm, the veins constrict and blood pressure increases, concentrating blood flow to the body core and brain where it's most needed during a confrontation (Siddle and Grossman, 1998).

The airways also dilate and we breathe quickly to increase our oxygen intake. This is adaptive because if we are stabbed or shot, we won't bleed to death as quickly and the remaining blood in our system will have higher levels of oxygen (Hole, 2001).

Muscles, Eyes and Blood Sugar

Muscle tension also increases, making the body stronger, faster and more resistant to penetrating wounds (Hole, 2001).

Pupils dilate to help identify threats, especially in low light. The stomach stops digesting and the body begins to increase the level of blood sugar and blood cholesterol to provide us with fuel in a timely manner.

The body also increases the level of cortisol, which processes energy sources and travels through the blood vessels to make them less permeable. Consequently, these blood vessels bleed or leak less easily when they become injured (Hole, 2001; McNally, 1999).

No Free Lunch

These effects are beneficial because they increase our ability to survive a violent encounter, but there is no such thing as a free lunch (Grossman, 2008). Chronic and prolonged stress causes blood sugar and blood cholesterol to remain high. Cortisol also damages blood vessel walls and over time can result in blocked arteries.

Tight muscles and dilated pupils can cause headaches. Hyperventilation can result in light-headedness. Chronic stress can cause white blood cells to diminish. Interference with stomach enzymes can cause diarrhea or constipation (Cunningham, 2002; Hole 2001).

Loss of Muscle Control

Another of the effects that occur when there is reduced blood flow to the extremities is loss of muscle control. At heart rates of 115 bpm, fine motor control begins to diminish. Heart rates between 115 and 145 bpm prime our system for survival, but we lose some fine motor skills, cognitive functions and gross motor functions, and our visual focus on the threat is heightened (Siddle and Grossman, 2008). Unless you are a sniper shooting at long range, you should welcome this.

As the stress response increases and our heart rate begins to exceed 145 bpm, hyper arousal begins to occur and our complex motor skills begin to deteriorate. What this means is that we can't load a magazine easily. It gets harder to change channels on a radio and we have trouble finding the transmission button on a mitre.

At heart rates of 175 bpm and above, the body prepares for a catastrophic reaction. The only things that work well are our gross motor functions. We can run, grapple and might be able to strike somewhere on a person's body with a baton, but shooting with any accuracy will be extremely difficult because our hands will begin to tremble involuntarily. In fact when heart rates exceed 175 bpm, most people would be lucky to hit the side of a barn.

Keep in mind that these reactions take place once the heart rate hits 175 bpm, but during a violent encounter, our sustained heart rate can remain at over 200 bpm for an extended period of time.

Reflexes Kick In

One other critical experience that occurs when the heart rate exceeds 175 bpm: our mature thinking brain begins to shut down and our reflexive brain begins to kick in (Siddle and Grossman, 2008).

The forebrain is the civilized, rational and sophisticated part of the brain that can engage in logical problem-solving behaviour. However, when the forebrain shuts down, the midbrain begins to take over. This brain area controls the reflex centres, and it is the more primitive system.

Good use-of-force trainers know that officers use the midbrain when we are in a violent confrontation. That's why they train you repeatedly until things are automatic. You pull your weapon and shout, "Police. Don't move!" over and over again until it is automatic and you can do it in your sleep.

That's important because when the heart rate hits 175 bpm and above, you don't think, you just react with reflexive behaviour.

Peripheral Vision Disappears

When in this state, peripheral vision begins to disappear and tunnel vision results. The actual shape of the eye begins to change and depth perception begins to alter. This can make the bad guy look extremely close. Often other stimuli, such as fellow officers who are responding along side us during a critical event, are tuned out.

Auditory Exclusion

Perceptual changes can also be accompanied by auditory exclusion processes. Use-of-force trainers repeatedly emphasize this phenomenon, which is often experienced by officers during a critical incident (Bremner, J. personal communication Sept. 2006).

It has great survival value because when officers are faced with a serious threat, the majority of energy is channelled to the senses that you need most (Grossman, 2008). During a violent encounter, the primary sense you need is vision. Therefore your brain processes visual stimuli well, but this occurs at the expense of the other senses. This is why gunshots sound loud when you observe an encounter, but seemingly disappear when you are the one who is involved in a shooting.

Sense of Touch Diminishes

The sense of touch often diminishes as well. Once we begin to focus on visual information and exclude other forms of sensory information, also called sensory gating, we can lose not only our sense of touch but our ability to respond to temperature and pain. It can also cause us to misperceive our actions during a critical incident because we lose muscle feedback that might tell us how hard we have been struck, or how hard we may have struck another person. This explains why an officer may perceive that he or she hardly struck a perpetrator during an encounter when in fact he or she may have broken the suspect's arm during an arrest.

Memory Affected

Similar perceptual distortions can take place involving memory. It is not uncommon for police officers to experience Critical Stress Amnesia following an event (Laur, 2002).

During a traumatic event the brain is focused on survival and not on accurately capturing memories. An officer may lose the ability to recall significant parts of an event immediately after it occurs. In many instances, the memories of parts of the event will be lost forever.

Altered Perceptions

In a 2006 study by Kevin Siddle, an expert on the psychology of police combat, officers were exposed to a simulated violent encounter.

The officers were led to believe that they could be injured during the experiment and were asked to sign a waiver releasing the experimenters from liability in the event of their death. This was done to increase the officers' stress level.

The officers were then confronted by a violent offender and their responses to this encounter were recorded while various aspects of the encounter were manipulated (for example, a loud air horn was set off during the experiment in order to assess for auditory exclusion). The experimenters asked the officers to evaluate their performance, and this was compared to objective data that was gathered during the experiment.

The following table shows some of the data.

Police responses to a simulated violent encounter

Shots fired	perceived 8.26	actual 12.71
Targets hit	perceived 4.38	actual 3.30
Accuracy	perceived 53%	actual 24.41%
Hesitation	perceived 26.19%	actual 10.42%
Fear/panic	perceived 4.76%	actual 16.67%
Auditory exclusion	perceived 23.81%	actual 58.33%

Source: Kevin Siddle, 2006

These data illustrate that an officer's perceptions of an event can differ dramatically from the objective event. It is interesting to note that the officers fired 50 per cent more shots but hit fewer targets than they thought. They also appeared to display more fear and panic than initially perceived, but even though more than one in four officers felt they hesitated to react, the data suggest that this did not occur as often as perceived. It is interesting to note that more than half of the officers failed to hear the loud horn during the confrontation, but only one in four recognized that auditory exclusion had taken place.

Perception and Reality

A failure to recognize and cope with these hormonally induced events can contribute to a stress reaction following a violent confrontation. Jimmy Bremner and I dealt with one young officer who was nearly beaten to death by an emotionally disturbed person who had escaped from a local hospital.

During the incident, the officer called for backup, but he perceived that no one had responded to his call. He was also upset because he felt he had failed to respond appropriately to the attack, for example, he had struck the attacker lightly with his baton, had failed to pull his weapon and had stood by idly as the attacker began his assault. However, additional data from the 911 call centre, fellow officers, witness reports and photographs taken following the assault showed a very different picture. It appears that the officer's calls for help were answered immediately and at least 10 officers marked on to the call within seconds. The event actually lasted less than two minutes from the start of the attack to the arrest of the subject by fellow officers.

Witness reports and photographic evidence also suggest that the young officer responded quickly, decisively and appropriately. He struck the attacker repeatedly with his fists and baton, he drew his firearm and despite the fact that the attacker was much larger than the officer, the attacker had suffered numerous serious injuries during the confrontation.

However, the officer continued to berate himself for hesitating to react and he harboured much anger toward his colleagues because he perceived that they had abandoned him during the assault.

As Jimmy discussed this with him, it became apparent that his reaction was one that was marked by auditory exclusion. For example, he could not hear responses on his mitre. He also suffered Critical Incident Amnesia and numerous other perceptual disturbances. Once this became apparent, his stress reaction diminished significantly.

Knowing What to Expect

Many officers are unaware that these hormonally induced effects take place because they do not generally occur during training exercises. That's because in a controlled environment stress hormones are not secreted, even though the heart rate may be elevated.

In a real life and death struggle, an officer's stress hormones begin to flow and these characteristic responses begin to occur. Officers need to know what to expect so they don't think they are losing control, which can fuel an overwhelming sense of shame or a perception that one has failed.

Psychological Effects of Combat

A number of psychological effects are associated with exposure to a violent encounter, the first one being fear. An officer who is attacked by an emotionally disturbed person may come to fear not only the original attacker, but all emotionally disturbed people. The officer may also come to fear hospitals in general, television programs involving hospitals, or sounds or smells that remind him or her of emotionally disturbed people, hospitals or related stimuli.

The officer may also come to have a fear response when he or she puts on a police uniform, straps on a duty belt or socializes with colleagues.

For an officer who is attacked on duty, close contact with another human being may become fear inducing. It is as though the brain says, "Be careful because something bad is going to happen." This may contribute to an uncontrollable urge to avoid sleeping with one's spouse or to avoid displays of affection with family members. This can cause the officer to conclude that he or she is losing control and "going crazy." It can also contribute to high levels of familial discord because family members don't understand what is happening.

It's easy to forget how your behaviour affects your family. For insight about what they might be going through, see Chapter 9.

Can't Avoid the Problem

Avoiding some anxiety-provoking work situations might be extremely difficult, and if attempts at avoidance begin to falter, some officers may turn to drugs or alcohol in order to calm their inner torment and to turn off the alarm reaction.

The brain is programmed to set off the alarm reaction whenever it encounters anything it believes might be harmful, and fighting this reaction is impossible. We must keep in mind that the alarm is inherently adaptive. The only thing that has gone wrong is that the brain has become far too sensitive to threat. This is extremely common following a serious critical incident.

Other Problems Associated with PTSD

Of all of those diagnosed with PTSD, 80 to 98.8 per cent struggle with at least one other clinical issue (Fairbank, Ebert and Caddell, 2001; McNally, 1999) including panic attacks, depression, substance abuse, anger and irritability.

Vicarious traumatization, which refers to PTSD symptoms that develop in spouses and children of officers involved in a traumatic event, is another issue.

Preventing and Treating PTSD in Police

The best way to prevent PTSD is through education. Know what to expect and where to get help. PTSD can be treated (cf. Fairbank, Ebert and Caddell, 2001) but in order to do so effectively, it must be diagnosed early. Otherwise, the condition can be very difficult to resolve, and in some cases the officer may never fully recover.

The first thing that we can do to reduce the effects of PTSD is to take it out of the closet. We need to demystify it. It is not a sign of weakness.

If you think you, or someone you know, may be showing signs of PTSD, it is important to find a trained medical health professional quickly. The longer you wait for treatment, the longer the treatment will take.

The second thing we can do is to provide stress inoculation training (SIT) programs. Ideally, these programs teach recruits what is normal when they deal with a violent encounter, since a lack of knowledge can lead to traumatic stress symptoms. SIT programs help recruits to identify these normal reactions and help them recognize signs of more serious PTSD so they can get help while they can still benefit from it. By teaching officers how to respond to critical incidents, we can greatly reduce their emotional and physical stress.

Third, we need to embed mental health professionals within police units. The U.S. military has done a great job with this. Psychologists have been embedded with fighting units. It is easier for the soldiers to seek treatment from people they are already familiar with from training exercises and social situations. Jimmy and I have personally had officers contact us because we've been involved with them in hockey leagues, tactical training exercises or through social activities organized by police associations. These officers, long before they encounter a traumatic incident, come to trust that they can count on our support. They are more likely to contact us if they know us personally and that we are available at any time.

When PTSD Strikes

When PTSD does develop, it's important that a trained mental health professional be contacted quickly, because untreated, PTSD can lead to chemical and structural changes in the brain.

These problems can be treated effectively through the use of a three-stage model developed by psychiatrist Judith Herman (Herman, 1997). Officers are taught to use safety strategies to control symptoms such as depression, panic attacks and nausea. Breathing strategies, relaxation, education regarding PTSD and the recovery process, along with the use of medications, are ways to achieve safety.

In the next stage, officers recall their trauma in a safe and effective manner while they are calm and relaxed.

It is a specialized process that allows the officer to learn that thinking about, dreaming about or talking about the incident is quite different from experiencing it. This essentially helps reset the brain's alarm system so it does not activate when confronted with innocuous stimuli. Over time, with the help of a trained professional, this can lead to the return to a healthy and normal lifestyle.

Restoring the Connection Between the Officer and Others

Psychological treatments, such as cognitive restructuring exercises and systematic desensitization procedures, are designed to normalize these experiences and can help to return the officer to his or her normal level of adaptive daily functioning fairly quickly.

However, in the final stage of therapy, the goal is to return the officer to a new sense of what is normal. In this stage, the officer is assisted in finding a way to reconnect with family members, peers and "everyday life" (Herman, 1997). The goal is also to ensure that feelings of safety can generalize so that the officer can return to regular, unrestricted work duties and a normal home life. Indeed, when therapy is done properly, many officers return to their duties with a renewed sense of confidence in themselves and their abilities.

Autogenic Breathing

It is important to note that once treatment ends, an officer may occasionally experience reflexive feelings of fear or symptoms of autonomic system arousal. When these characteristic responses occur, they can be reduced by using autogenic breathing, a simple technique that has been used by military and tactical trainers for years to reduce the heart rate by up to 30 per cent (Laur, 2002).

Unfortunately, despite its potential to save lives, these simple techniques are often taught only to officers on tactical units.

In order to use autogenic breathing, you merely have to slow your breathing pattern by using "belly breaths" (diaphragmatic breathing). You can do this simply by breathing in for a count of four, holding your breath for a count of four, breathing out for a count of four, then holding your breath for a count of four. Continue to repeat this process and you will notice that your heart rate begins to slow and muscle tension begins to diminish. This can be done even in a very stressful situation.

You must remember to hold your breath for a count of four when you breathe in, then again when you breathe out. This allows the oxygen and carbon dioxide levels to balance and prevents many stress-related effects associated with hyper-arousal and hyper-ventilation.

Be Prepared

Stress may trigger a relapse and PTSD sufferers may need additional help in the future. It's important to maintain relationships with your doctor and support group.

9

A Note from Home
By Dayle Bremner

Jim and I met in early 1980 at the El Mocambo tavern in downtown Toronto. We were both fans of live music and would run into each other from time to time at clubs when our favourite bands were playing. What impressed me about him was his quiet, gentle manner. He was also a true gentleman, very respectful of people and had a great sense of humor. We married in 1981. He joined the police service in 1986, and we had a son in 1987 and a daughter in 1989.

When he was hired by the police service I remember wondering if the job would change him. Most police officers I had known had been cynical people, not at all like Jim, and I couldn't imagine him ever becoming like that. But over the years, I have come to realize that policing can take a terrible toll on those who are sworn to serve and protect.

During the first few years on the job Jim would come home with stories about what had occurred on his shift. Some were hilarious and others were quite sad or disturbing – but he did share his experiences with me, and I think it gave me some understanding of what his days and nights were like out on the road. We enjoyed an active social life that included friends from police and civilian circles and we would often get together with his co-workers and their families for dinners, trips with the kids to the zoo, children's birthday parties and other family events. It was wonderful to see the camaraderie between Jim and the guys he worked with. Jim seemed very happy.

After he joined SWAT, he didn't talk much about his work any more. I felt like I had to pry to get information from him. Communicating with his co-workers didn't seem to be a problem for him, though. I would overhear him talking on the phone and he always had a lot to say to them. I have to admit that I was a little jealous when I heard him talking and laughing with one of the guys on his team. This exclusion bothered me a lot. Trying to talk to Jim about the lack of communication was futile. He would just say, "I don't want to burden you with the horrible things that I see."

But, other than the lack of communication about his work, Jim was a great guy and a good husband and father, so I just went along with things as they were.

Over time, I noticed he was becoming a little tense and short tempered. He was going out for drinks with his buddies from work more often. His behaviour was changing, but it was so gradual that I rationalized it as being normal for someone with varied shifts and such a demanding job. In retrospect, these were clues that I could have picked up on if I had known what to look for, or had understood the cumulative effects of stress.

Then there was New Year's Eve 1999/2000, the St. Michael's Hospital incident, when Jim shot and killed a man who had taken a doctor hostage. Since he had to work I took the kids and went to spend the night at a friend's place to ring in the New Year. The next morning I saw a story in the newspaper about police shooting a man at St. Michael's Hospital and called home right away. Jim told me that he had been involved. I left the kids at my friend's house and headed home. Before leaving, I told them, "Dad has been involved in a shooting. You know your Dad. If he shot someone, it's because he had to. Whatever happens, you know Dad."

I wasn't sure what to expect when I got home – would there be reporters and television cameras on the front lawn? Thankfully, all was quiet when I pulled up to the house. I found Jim, asleep in the basement, still groggy after having downed a few drinks when he was finally allowed to return home after the horrible events of the previous night.

There was a lot of negative media and criticism directed at Jim and the police service in the weeks and months that followed the shooting. Our family tried, as best we could, to continue on with our daily lives, but we were overwhelmed and felt very isolated. It was a difficult time for our children; they were put in the position of having to respond to people's questions and comments. For me, it felt as if I was living a bad dream. I can't even imagine what was going on in Jim's head; I did not realize the depth of the effect this was having on him. The whole family should have been in counselling but we weren't. Looking back now I feel that we all would have benefitted from crisis counselling immediately after the incident.

As time went on, Jim was becoming even more stressed. He was quick to lose his temper, slept a lot and grew more reclusive. He would say, "Why would I want to go out? I deal with people all day and I just want to stay home and watch TV." His drinking was increasing. He would often down two or three drinks when others would have only one. He seemed to need alcohol in order to relax.

I missed the company of my husband. The children tried to steer clear of him but it was obvious they missed the time they used to share with their father. If there were any arguments or squabbles in the house, Jim would react, imploring, "If you don't stop, I'm going to get sick."

I found myself angry almost all of the time. Angry at Jim for his behaviour and angry at management for not supporting him as well as I thought they could have. I came to realize much later that my fear, anxiety, loneliness, grief and helplessness were being translated into anger.

This was our life until the inquest into the St. Michael's Hospital shooting was over, about 18 months later.

Although Jim was vindicated at the inquest in April/May 2001, the strain of this whole experience had taken its toll on our entire family. Without receiving appropriate support, and not having the capacity or knowledge about where to find help, we continued in this negative spiral and the stress accumulated.

By the spring of 2004, I was convinced that Jim was an alcoholic, or on his way to becoming one. It hadn't even occurred to me that he might have PTSD. I insisted that he make an appointment to see his doctor and take me along, as I didn't trust him to tell the doctor what was really going on.

We saw the doctor, an excellent physician who Jim had been seeing since he was 12 years old. Jim didn't look well. He looked worn out. I said to the doctor, "I think Jim is an alcoholic. What can we do about it?"

The doctor responded, saying, "Dayle, he's not an alcoholic. He's struggling with PTSD and is self-medicating. The alcohol has the same calming effect that medication for PTSD would have."

I was furious. How could he say Jim wasn't an alcoholic? I lived with the drinking; I saw how often he was coming home drunk. I had been pleading with Jim to stop, but he just brushed me off. My understanding of PTSD was very limited, and I never saw any indication that Jim was having flashbacks. That was my idea of what PTSD was – flashbacks. Now I know that there are many other symptoms of PTSD. Jim had many: irritability, impatience, sleeplessness, difficulty concentrating, exaggerated startle reflex, isolation and increased consumption of alcohol.

Jim was to see a psychiatrist and go back to the doctor in 10 days for a follow-up appointment. The doctor had him promise that in the meantime he would not drink and drive. Sadly, within those 10 days, Jim was found by police – drunk and passed out behind the wheel of a car on the side of Highway 401.

He had been out of town giving a seminar to another police service a couple of hours away and had called around dinnertime to say he was going to stay for a while to spend some time with "the guys." Much later when I tried to reach him on his cell phone it was turned off. I knew that when his phone was off, it often meant he was drinking. I immediately went into a panic; I was worried sick about him and felt very helpless because I was not able to reach him. It was a long and sleepless night.

Early the next morning the commanding officer of Jim's unit phoned and informed me, rather bluntly, that Jim had been arrested for impaired driving. He stated that it would be a long time before Jim would be back on a team. After the phone call, I realized that he never said how Jim was. Was he in a car accident? Was he hurt? I had been too stunned by the news to even ask. I called the station back to find out and was told that there had not been an accident. Thank God for that!

A few hours later I received a call from one of his buddies from work who had been sent to get Jim. He was letting me know that Jim was extremely upset and feeling bad about the whole mess. "Please don't be too hard on him, Dayle; he's already beating himself up as it is." When they pulled up at the house, I went outside. Jim walked right past me, head down, ashamed to look at me. As he passed by he said, "Why don't you just file for divorce?" He looked absolutely terrible. I was relieved to see him and to have him back at home.

After the incident on the highway, it was as if Jim had lost all hope. Finally all the hardship and stress of the past five years hit. The Employee and Family Assistance Program put him in touch with Dr. Sean P. O'Brien, a clinical psychologist who specializes in officers with PTSD. Jim was in such bad shape for the first six to eight months that I was seriously worried for his life. He would leave the house and walk for hours and hours, often along the railroad tracks. I was worried that he would be hit by a train either accidentally or on purpose. I was living in a constant state of anxiety and hypervigilance, and eventually saw a psychologist for a few appointments myself. I thought that once Jim got into treatment, I would be fine, but the effects of coping with the turmoil in our lives did not disappear as I thought they would. Again, I just continued along trying to take care of Jim and the kids. Someone had to step up to the plate and look after things — I could not afford to be weak.

Jim was seeing Dr. O'Brien a few times each week, but progress was very slow. He continued to drink and would go missing for hours on end, turning off his cell phone so he couldn't be reached. I spent many nights driving around to bars looking for him. I begged him to stop drinking. I pleaded. I threatened. I screamed. I ranted and raved. I almost ripped his t-shirt right off of him one night, trying to shake some sense into him.

Finally, in January 2005, a spot became available for Jim in a PTSD program. Entering the program would mean he would be away from home for two months of treatment. He didn't want to go, but by this time I was ready to give up on him and file for divorce, and he knew it. Reluctantly, he agreed to give it a try.

It was a huge relief for me to finally have him in treatment and I was glad that our children would be spared the chaos that we had been living with for the past few years.

They say you never know who your true friends are until you're in a crisis. Most people we knew vanished, either because they didn't know what to do or say or because they really just didn't care. Some special people from his team were wonderful. They called me, some stopped by the house to make sure I was all right when Jim was away at rehab and one even stayed on the phone and listened to me cry when I was just too upset to speak. I will never forget these people.

Our family was under a great deal of stress. Police Act charges had been filed for discreditable conduct relating to the impaired driving, making things even worse. It was a time when Jim was at the lowest point in his life. He was found guilty of discreditable conduct and as punishment had to forfeit 17 days of pay, a ruling that affected not only Jim but the children and me as well. We were struggling financially with Jim not being able to take on paid duties and my being unable to work as much as I used to because of a bad back. I still cannot understand why the service pursued the Police Act charges knowing that Jim had been diagnosed with work-related PTSD.

At some point, not long after he completed the PTSD program, he stopped drinking. It took a few years before I could begin to trust him again so whenever he would come home after being out I would try to discreetly smell his breath. I was paranoid and expecting a relapse. The smell of any type of alcohol, even mouthwash or hand sanitizer, would send me into a panic. Now I don't worry about him drinking; I know he's not an alcoholic.

Jim still struggles with symptoms of PTSD on a daily

basis but the symptoms are nowhere near as severe as they once were. He will never be as well as he was before Post Traumatic Stress Disorder but with the help of his psychologist he has learned coping strategies. I also struggle with anxiety and anger related to his illness, although less often as time has passed.

This experience with PTSD has had a profound and lasting effect on our whole family. Our son and daughter, now young adults, have grown up with a father who was emotionally absent and in crisis for much of their lives – and this has changed them. They are more distant than they were, more guarded with their feelings. It has affected our sense of stability as a family and has put so much strain on the marriage that I am amazed we are still together. There are still days when I'm not sure we can make it. I wouldn't wish this on anyone.

Lessons Learned

Policing is stressful. PTSD is an occupational hazard. When one family member is suffering with PTSD, the whole family suffers.

With proper intervention, perhaps many cases of PTSD can be avoided, or the debilitating effects lessened. I feel that it is incumbent on every employer to take any and all steps necessary to safeguard the health of their employees.

What is needed is genuine care and concern for officers out there on the front lines every day doing a tremendously stressful, dangerous, often thankless job. There are lives at stake; families are hurting and children are being affected. Take a good, hard look around. Do you know officers who drink heavily? What about the number of failed marriages? Know anyone who is tense, argumentative and quick to anger? And what about yourself? Is your wife bitching at you? Having trouble at home? These are symptoms that something is wrong!

So why are many police officers suffering in silence? Officers need to feel that it is safe to ask for help. What they don't need is to worry about being judged, losing their jobs or being demoted to another position if they seek help. They have worked hard to get where they are. They have families to feed and mortgages to pay. To stigmatize them is to push them underground, where the problem only festers. Remember, the earlier the intervention the greater likelihood of a quicker recovery.

Speaking with a psychologist should be a normal part of a career in policing – not something reserved for "mental cases." Why wait until someone is in crisis before getting help? And why, in this day and age, does seeking help carry a stigma?

I would like to see every police employee, from the chief down, get ongoing training in Critical Incident Stress/PTSD. Spouses and children of police officers should be included. Articles outlining the symptoms to be aware of and steps to take should be distributed regularly to police families to ensure that no one misses the information.

All I know is that our police officers and their families deserve better than they are currently getting. We need to be educated. We need to be kinder and look out for each other. And we need to learn that asking for help is not a sign of weakness.

They say, "You can't fix what you won't acknowledge." Police services need to acknowledge that PTSD in policing is a serious issue and that steps need to be taken to ensure that any person struggling with symptoms gets the help he or she needs.

And most importantly, I would like all police officers and their families to know that it is absolutely normal to have difficulties coping with the stresses they are dealing with. Please know that there are people who understand and are willing to help. Ask for the help you need, and keep asking, even demanding, until you get it.

10

A Note from the Sergeant's Desk
By Sgt. Mike Babineau
Special Weapons Team One, retired

Countless times, Jimmy Bremner stepped up to the plate and did what he was trained to do. The St. Michael's Hospital shooting in Toronto in the early minutes of 2000, when my team rescued a doctor being held hostage by a father demanding immediate attention for his infant, had a huge impact – not only on Jimmy, one of two who actually pulled the trigger, but also on Jimmy's wife, his children and the rest of my team. To make matters worse, we found out after the fact that the suspect's weapon was a pellet gun.

As a team, we all knew what we might have to do on that day. We had trained countless hours for such calls so that when the day came we would be prepared and ready to deal with any situation that might confront us, including a hostage rescue. But when that call ended with a shooting, it affected every member of the team. Some will admit it, some won't, but it changed us. The St. Michael's Hospital call changed everything.

Let me tell you about Team One. It was a collection of 10 of the finest officers you could find. We had people from the four corners of the city. We had people who excelled in different areas and possessed specific expertise, and as a result, we fed off of each other. What we had in common was that we wanted to be the best we could be. Because we all had the drive to be the best, we were labelled by some of our supervisors and co-workers as being overzealous. They didn't like it because we did things differently from how they had always been done. We always tried to find a more efficient way to meet our objectives.

Team One would come in, get our weapons ready for the day and get everything set just in case. Then we would go to the gym, do our workout, get showered and then sit down and plan and discuss what would be done that day. We were prepared to answer a call from the time we started each shift because calls could come in at any time. I always preferred to be prepared.

Team One's protocol was to bring all of our gear with us for each call rather than to have to go back to the trucks if we needed something. To make this easier, each of us purchased a load-bearing vest. It was a lot easier to have all our gear on the vest at the ready. When we stood down, we could take the vest and the equipment off all at once then put it all on at once when necessary. We wore our vests on patrol, reasoning that there was no point in getting to a call and then saying, hang on while I put on my gear. It doesn't work that way. So that's what we would do. We would go to a call, roll up and be ready.

I actually had a superior comment that every time we left the station we left dressed for war, and it wasn't meant as a compliment. It was a criticism. We weren't dressed for war, we were dressed to do our jobs.

Team One loved to train. The focal point of Team One was Jimmy. The team revolved around Jimmy, and Jimmy revolved around the team. Ultimately I had control, but I trusted him implicitly to make sure that we did things right, that we had the tools to do them right and that what we did we did safely so everyone came home at the end of the day.

We would meet at the train yard on midnights one rotation, trading a training day for a training night. For that, willingly working midnights, we struck a sour note with some of the other teams. What the hell were we thinking? We went to an unused subway station and practiced sniper initiated assaults, how to breach a subway car, moving from cover to cover on the platform – any scenario we could think of relating to the subway. On evenings we went to the streetcar garage and did the same thing with streetcars. We did all sorts of different training on our own. We were chastised by the unit as a whole, including some management, because this type of training was "outside the box."

We wanted to figure out how to get on to a school bus in case we ever had a hostage situation. Once again we were labelled by some as being overzealous. It would never happen, we were told. Shortly thereafter, down in the United States, a school bus was taken hostage. We knew how to render the situation safe. We had already figured that out.

We thought it would be prudent if we learned how to assault the Toronto Island ferry. Some of the supervisors looked at us as if we all had two heads. We made it happen anyway. We teamed up with the marine unit and devised a plan to get on to the boat. It worked flawlessly.

These training events took place in the late 1990s. By the early 2000s much of what we did and were criticized for doing had become standard operating procedure. Load-bearing vests were standard issue. Members participated in waterborne assault courses. School bus assaults were part of the tactical course. Everything that we did that caused us to be labelled rogue is now standard procedure. My team, that unique group of officers, was just five years ahead of its time.

The second-guessing by some untrusting supervisors continued and put a terrible stress on everyone. Jimmy especially took great exception to the constant criticism and it began to wear him down little by little.

But we continued to do the best that we could. That's the type of guys we were, willing to train and go the extra mile, and that's the type of guys who make Team One to this day. I see current Team One members that I have never worked with, that Jimmy has never worked with, yet they come up to me and assure me that they are keeping the standards that we set for them. The original Team One set the bar extremely high. Jimmy was the one who orchestrated the setting of the bar. All he wanted to do was to make sure everybody got the highest level of training possible.

You will never find a man more dedicated, more loyal to his craft than Jimmy Bremner.

I knew that from the first time I saw him on a call in 1992. Jimmy and I hit it off right away. He did things directly, with no beating around the bush, just like I like to operate – straight and to the point.

For some strange reason, fate I suppose, we crossed paths on a regular basis for the next while and shortly thereafter, I made my move to SWAT. I went to the unit very senior, 42 years old, which in itself is fairly rare. It's mostly younger guys there. I had virtually no tactical experience, making my move even more unusual.

A new SWAT constable gets to do the basic tactical orientation course and learns from the fringes for as long as it takes him to move into the line-up. I was going in as a sergeant. I didn't have that luxury. I went on the basic tactical course and the day after the course ended, I was commanding a gun team.

Jimmy and I were not on the same team but our friendship grew and the bond strengthened and developed into the relationship that we have today. I didn't work with him until the spring of 1997. Once we were on the same team, we put our philosophy to work. Jimmy and I would never let a window of opportunity pass. If you don't take advantage of an opportunity, you might never get it back again. If we had the chance to end a call safely, we did.

We didn't like to talk for hours and let the suspect take control of the situation and to dictate the outcome. At any given second, the bad guy can change the direction of the call to go from calm to suicidal or violent. I can't and wouldn't give the bad guy that option. If we had the opportunity to reach in and grab him, you could consider him grabbed. That was our philosophy. Subsequently, a lot of our calls ended very quickly. We watched for the subject to make a mistake, which gave us an opening to end the call safely and efficiently.

The majority of our calls ended safely for everyone involved, but the two that didn't were fugitive Tyrone Conn in a basement on Alberta Avenue and Henry Masuka at St. Michael's Hospital. In both calls, it was the suspect who dictated the outcome.

Tyrone Conn was calm, in control and talking on a cell phone. We were waiting for him to hang up and come out of the basement, which is what he had agreed to do. Tyrone Conn dictated the outcome when he took his own life. His death was ruled a suicide. Media scrutiny was extensive and had a tremendous effect on the team.

The next call that ended unfavourably for the suspect was at St Michael's Hospital. Communications were going fine when, for reasons unknown, Henry Masuka dictated the outcome. He told us this is going to end right now and moved toward the doctor in a threatening manner. That was our window of opportunity. The difference between that window of opportunity and the others was that this call required lethal force. But we had no choice. It had to be ended.

The doctor and the baby were rescued successfully but that didn't seem to matter. In the media, the team was accused of everything from planting the gun to ensuring the incident happened out of the view of hospital security cameras. The media attention comes with the job but it wasn't so much the publicity, as the lack of support from the service that hurt and got us, and in particular Jimmy, down. It was the lack of understanding from some of the people we worked with and for.

About 18 months later, we were exonerated of any wrongdoing in the St. Michael's shooting. It's probably the only inquest that the police have been involved in as a principal party where a recommendation wasn't brought down against them. Not a one. It was picture perfect, if you can say a call like that can be perfect. There is nothing more that we could have done that would have changed the outcome.

The lack of recognition and support affected the guys. We won't downplay it in any way shape or form. The St. Mike's call was an incredible, traumatic 18 minutes. You can't begin to comprehend all the stuff that went down. We arrived at 11:45 and at 12:03 the suspect was dead. Ironically, 1203 was my badge number.

After the Tyrone Conn call, during which the team faced a man with a loaded shot gun and put themselves in great danger, the chief was at the unit two days later and called us in and told us we did a great job. He even went as far as to assure me they were behind me 100 per cent and not to pay attention to the articles written in the papers.

The media had dumped all over me, saying that we went in and shot the guy. We had a great plan that would have worked had the suspect not deviated from the agreed upon plan and changed the outcome. That was a great call but it still weighed heavily on Jimmy's mind that he couldn't save the suspect from himself.

Post Traumatic Stress Disorder doesn't always happen because of a single event, but a single event can bring PTSD to the surface. That's the way I see it. With Jimmy, I don't think it was the act of pulling the trigger at St. Mike's or being unable to save Conn from himself. I think it was the aftermath, that lack of recognition and understanding.

These experiences don't just disappear at the end of the day; they sit there and they build up. The anxiety and emotion begin to rot you from the inside out. Then something happens and you explode. It's like a balloon being filled with air. It becomes larger and larger, then all of a sudden it bursts.

Jimmy's emotional balloon was filling quickly, soon to be stretched to the limit. The hard part in all of this is that I wasn't there at the time Jimmy really began to have problems. I had been given the opportunity to go to the police college to be a firearms instructor. I left the unit in October 2000, 10 months after the St. Mike's incident. Jimmy was in the training office and the team had been broken up.

I accept a tremendous amount of the blame for what happened to Jimmy. I was there and he was my friend and I didn't do anything. On many occasions, I had told people that I thought he was suffering from these incidents. Jimmy himself told me that it was affecting him badly. He said he told others of the effect it was having on him. They didn't do anything and neither did I.

If I could go back 10 years, I would go back 10 years and change it. I would start in the minutes after the suspect was shot and not stop until I was sure that all of us received the attention and care required. There were steps I should have taken but didn't.

I can't help but wonder where we would be now if I had.

Some of us didn't leave the station until 11:30 or 12 the morning of Jan. 1. The boss asked if the team was coming in that night. I said no, we're not coming in. I knew enough that we shouldn't be coming back the next night.

On Jan. 3 we had to come in and do our notes and be interviewed by investigators. We were walking down the hall and the unit commander says, "So what's up Mike? Are you guys coming back to work?" Before I could say, "No," all of the guys on the team, except for Jimmy, said, "Yeah we'll be in tonight." I was thinking something is wrong with this. I should have stood up and said I don't care what you think, I'm the team sergeant and we are standing down. But I didn't. We came back the next night and there was another shooting. In a struggle with team members, a gun discharged and a suspect was wounded. Soon afterwards, they broke apart our team and gave us different assignments, which did not help our recovery process. Jimmy especially mourned the loss of the team. If I had stood my ground, what might have been?

Some time later, Jimmy went to management and said, "I'm having a hard time with this." Jimmy was sarcastically told, "Yeah we're all having a rough time." Management did nothing. To make matters worse, Jimmy came to me at the college and told me what had been said. I still didn't do anything.

I think stigma comes into play. As a sergeant, as a supervisor, I should have sent Jimmy to get help, but as a friend I didn't want to accept the fact that there was a problem. I didn't want to have him labelled, to have the stigma of being weak. That didn't make me much of a friend.

The balloon became larger and larger over the next couple of years, threatening Jimmy's very existence. It was frightening to think that a tactical officer could be brought down by something like Post Traumatic Stress. If Jimmy Bremner could fall, then everyone was susceptible.

I remember talking to a sergeant who was on a course with Jimmy. They had shared a hotel room and he told me the story of Jimmy's nightmares. This sergeant told me he sat in the corner crying as he watched Jimmy suffering through them. Once again, I did nothing and I feel guilty and regretful to this day. If there was something I could do to make it up to Jimmy, I would.

The body has incredible mechanisms that it uses to cope. When it gets overwhelmed it shuts down, blocks everything out and fails to function. You lose the ability to make rational and sound decisions. You see everything and everyone as being against you. That's when you have to get help.

That's what happened to Jimmy. All of his coping mechanisms had failed. That's when he ended up sleeping in the backyard and on the street, and doing all the unusual things he was doing. He was a wreck, a mental and physical wreck. Jimmy Bremner had hit rock bottom.

They say you can't begin the journey back, you can't pull yourself up, until you hit bottom. My Jimmy was gone and he had been replaced by someone with no resemblance to the man I knew and cared about so deeply.

It was a very hard and emotional day, the day we drove to rehab to begin his recovery process, but I knew if anyone could rebound, it would be Jimmy. He has an uncanny determination when it comes to seeing an objective and reaching a goal. He's the type of individual who, when he realizes what has to be done, will pull out all the stops to make it happen. I never had any doubt he'd be able to do it. He just needed to recognize what was wrong and how to get better. If you don't recognize or admit to the disease, how can you find the cure?

It's hard work to get better. It's easier to go out and get drunk than it is to not drink. I would hear stories about the drinking and parties from the team the day after a night at the bar and how Jimmy went over the top with his drinking.

I suppose by not stepping in and intervening, we just helped him down the path to the bottom and now that he was there it would be a long road back.

Post Traumatic Stress Disorder is not supposed to have an effect on your career. Unfortunately, people don't look at it as a disease; they look at it as a weakness. And being perceived as being weak is something that officers will go to any length to avoid. It has made Jimmy's recovery harder.

As for me, the anger caused by what happened to Jimmy and the team stayed with me for a long, long time. It was years before I could get past being bitter about all the things that happened while I was on Team One. For six years after I left SWAT, I couldn't drive down the highway and pass the cut-off I would have taken to get to work without getting angry. Now I know it's not worth it. The misery is not worth it, my health is more important. That's all behind me now. The only thing I won't put behind me is what happened to Jimmy.

Am I afraid that it will happen to me? There were and

still are times when I really have to take a step back and calm down. I think because I know what happened to Jimmy, I'm very much aware that it's possible I could travel down that same road. Recognition and understanding of the symptoms makes me better able to deal with PTSD. However, there are times – for example, when I talk about Jimmy and what happened – that I sometimes feel extremely guilty and overwhelmed. I trade those thoughts for thoughts of the good times we had and have to this day. It helps to relieve the anxiety.

I used to find myself thinking about the St. Mike's incident a lot. Not so much now. Every New Year's Eve I send an email to all the guys who were on the team wishing them the best and reassuring them of the high regard in which I hold them. This year I realized it was 10 years ago that it happened. It shouldn't even be on my mind. I can't remember what I did yesterday, but if I was an artist, I could draw you a detailed picture of what happened 10 years ago. Police officers, even retired officers, think they can handle it and that they don't need help, but ...

I've had one really bad episode where I thought I wouldn't be able to control it. Luckily it was brief. I was obsessed with the St. Mike's call. In my flashback, I heard Jimmy say to me, "I need to know my backstop." The suspect was sitting in front of a window that had a drywall partition behind it. That statement in itself shows the degree of professionalism Jimmy has. To have the presence of mind to want to know what was beyond the glass and drywall, behind the suspect, with all that was going on at the speed it was going on, was extraordinary. "I have to know what my backstop is in case I have a through and through (shot), or in case I miss," Jimmy said. I went out to investigate and found about 40 people standing right there, behind the wall. I moved all of those people and came back and told Jimmy he had a clear shot.

A little while later, the suspect made a threat and turned toward the doctor. Jimmy took the shot. I have no recollection of hearing it, or seeing the impact, or seeing Henry Masuka fall. It goes from Henry turning toward the doctor, to me entering the room where Henry was and seeing him lying on the floor. I had a very hard time with that. I thought I was going to lose my mind. Somehow, I managed to carry on. That's when I went to my doctor. When I told her I couldn't remember the details, she said something very profound. She said, "Why would you want to remember?" I looked at her and said, "You're probably right." Why do I want to have a vivid recollection of Henry Masuka dying in the manner he did? I was five feet away, yet I have no recollection. I remember everything leading up to the shot. I didn't even know my 2 I/C (second in command) shot him as well. I was focused on Jimmy. He and Jimmy both shot at the same time, both perceiving the same threat at the same time. Like I said, things affect people in different ways, to different degrees, with different outcomes. My 2 I/C was able to deal with it and his outcome was favourable.

This was just one call, adding to so much other horrible stuff. We've had to deal with people jumping off bridges, dead bodies, dismemberments, crushed bodies, all manner of horrific things. It has its effect. Some officers won't admit it, but it does. How can it not?

It's the stigma and the fear of how being diagnosed with

an illness like Post Traumatic Stress Disorder will affect a career that keeps officers from getting help.

As stated earlier, Post Traumatic Stress Disorder is not supposed to have an effect on your career, but unfortunately some people don't look at it as a disease; they look at it as a weakness. Being perceived as weak is something that officers will go to any length to avoid. However, is Post Traumatic Stress Disorder any worse than having a broken leg? You've got a broken spirit. You mend a leg and you have to take time to mend your spirit.

Hindsight is 20-20. I have learned the hard way.

Someone once said, and he must have been a very wise man, "Heroes are those people who do what has to be done when it needs to be done, regardless of the consequences." He was referring to my boys on Special Weapons Team One.

HOW TO SAVE A LIFE

1. When you see a friend or co-worker doing something that is out of the ordinary, or behaving out of character, don't ignore it. Find out why. Show him that you care and let him know you are there to help in any way he needs.

2. Don't be afraid to confront your friend with your feelings and fears. Tell him that he needs to seek help and you will be there for him. Don't take no for an answer.

3. Pursue your feelings regardless of the outcome and effect it will have on the relationship. If you don't, the relationship could end with a funeral. Better to lose the friendship than lose the friend.   — *M.B.*

11

A Note from the Writers' Desk
By Mark Ellis and Stephanie Morgenstern
co-creators of *Flashpoint*

Flashpoint's first day of filming took place in Commerce Court in July 2007, in the heart of downtown Toronto. When you've been developing a script for over two years, it's quite a feeling to walk onto the set for the first time. This was the pilot episode and we were shooting Sgt. Parker's standoff with Goran Tomasic – a tough negotiation because the gunman spoke no English. There were squad cars, an ambulance, a fire truck, *Flashpoint*'s SRU Suburbans and a command truck. There was the cast, wearing their tactical uniforms for the first time. A flock of background performers, looking very convincing as passers-by, news reporters, paramedics, plainclothes cops. The crew, who had completely taken over the public square. Hundreds of people. Seeing your script come true kind of blows your mind.

The first person we said hello to was an Emergency Task Force constable, dressed in tactical greys. Or at least we thought he was an ETF officer. It turned out he was an extra. The real cop was standing about 20 feet to our left, in civvies. It was Jimmy Bremner, and he was showing Sergio Di Zio (Spike) and Michael Cram (Wordy) how to hold their MP5s properly.

We cruised on by, letting them work. It wasn't until there was a gap in the filming, hours later, that we struck up a conversation with Jimmy. It was a conversation that shaped the show over the next 50 episodes …

Two years earlier there had been a shooting at Toronto's busy Union Station. A man took a young woman hostage in the middle of the morning rush hour, surrounded by hundreds of people. The officer negotiating that day did his best but was unable to reach the man, and when the man turned his weapon on the ETF, they were forced to shoot him. It was a shocking incident, one we're used to seeing happen in movies, not in real life. Not in your own city, not so close to where you live.

It got us thinking about the man who took a hostage that morning. About what might have driven him to do what he'd done. It got us thinking about his hostage, and how terrifying her experience must have been. But most of all, it got us thinking about the officer who had to take that fatal shot. It was 9:30 in the morning and an officer had just been asked to become a public executioner. Where is he right now? What's the rest of his day been like?

We thought about all the movies and TV shows we'd seen. All the stories about detectives, forensic investigators, beat cops, bad guys and hostage takers. Sometimes a SWAT team is called in. A faceless cop in black takes a shot. Someone pats him on the back. Everyone goes home. It can't be like that in real life. It's not.

Flashpoint started out as a two-hour TV movie script about a constable who's been trained to fire a sniper rifle but not prepared to kill a human being. It was about the rest of his day and the weeks that followed. It was about how hard it was for him to get over that shooting. As we developed that premise into a TV series, we found inspiration in the Toronto Emergency Task Force's record – they had used lethal force only nine times in over 40 years. We focused on a tactical team that was cross-trained in human behaviour assessment and psychological profiling. We wanted to write a show about a SWAT unit whose job it is to ask questions first and use weapons last and what the repercussions were when they did have to pull a trigger.

When we were developing the series, the question we were asked over and over again was: Why's it such a big deal to shoot someone? Isn't that part of a cop's job? It's an understandable question. The thing is, we're desensitized. We expect our cops to be able to kill casually, because we live in a culture where it's normal for forensic investigators on TV to shoot a couple of people in the afternoon and then forget about it by the time they reach for their evening cocktail. We'd pass along Jimmy Bremner's mantra: "Cops are trained to fire their weapon. They're not trained to kill people."

This is one of our driving ideas behind *Flashpoint:* the fact that killing is difficult – that it's a shock to the soul; that it haunts you, no matter how justified you believe it was – and that this is a good thing. It means you're still human. As horrific as the experience of taking a life may be, the true horror would be the moment it becomes easy.

We came face to face with the human cost of the job when we met Jimmy Bremner that day. Although he wasn't involved in the Union Station shooting, he had tales of his own to tell. He was a striking counterpoint to the alpha swagger and bravado we associated with other tactical cops. The difference hits you right away: here's a thoughtful, introspective man with a gentle voice, an open face and clear blue eyes that still shine with grief when he recounts the incidents that took him to such dark places. We were taken by surprise that he was willing to talk so openly the very first day we met him. At that time, those memories were all still fresh, the wounds far from healed. It's that fragile, vulnerable quality about Jimmy, a guy who's endured and survived, that made such a deep impression on us. We wanted to capture some of the kind of courage that must have taken, not only to struggle back onto your feet after falling, but also to tell that story so readily, so that others may not follow in your path.

There's one *Flashpoint* episode in the first season that's dedicated to that spirit. It's called *Haunting the Barn*, and it's the one closest to our hearts. In it, Danny Rangford, a legendary figure on the force, recently retired, comes to the station. This man was a hero to many, a mentor to our team leader Ed Lane. But on this day, he barricades himself in the briefing room, pulls out a bottle of scotch and a gun, and lays out, all over the floor, press clippings and other mementos from his long career.

Those were the public stories. It's the private stories behind them that have been slowly destroying him. The stories he's never been able to tell, because heroes aren't allowed flaws. He's not allowed to talk about the cost of those split-second decisions, made under pressure, the choices he'll never get a second chance at. About all the lives in his hands that he could have handled better. About how, over the years, he pushed away the woman who loved him … because he couldn't share this nightmare with her. Danny can't live with the ghosts any more and wants to end it all right there.

This episode is about the courage it takes for Ed Lane to step out from behind the shield, pull off the bulletproof vest and admit, in front of all his brothers-in-arms: I know those ghosts. I've seen them. You're not alone. For us, Jimmy's message comes down to something that simple: you're not alone. All we have to do is talk and tell the truth.

It's been a few years since that first conversation with Jimmy, and we've been lucky to have him by our side, helping us keep it real – as real as one can on network television.

We've also witnessed a change in him since that day. It's the change that comes with having found what you're meant to do: a task that reclaims all the troubles, losses and regrets, and wrestles them into a force that fights back. We're proud that our association with Jimmy on *Flashpoint* has been a part of that. And we're proud to see his book reach the rest of the world. Jimmy's story will change the way you look at a cop when you see him walking down the street.

12

A Call for Change

By S/Sgt. Barney McNeilly retired
president of Canadian Critical Incident Inc.

It's an awkward situation. Post Traumatic Stress Disorder is seen as a mental illness, and as such, management may look upon it as a weakness. And no officer wants to appear weak. An officer suspected of having, or diagnosed as having PTSD, would be taken off the job immediately and put on a desk or filing job. Their career would be finished, even if in five years they had a letter from their psychiatrist saying that they're perfectly capable of doing their job. That's the problem. It's no wonder no one wants to jeopardize their career by appearing weak or being seen coming out of a psychiatrist's office or asking for help.

In 1965, I started my policing career by joining the Royal Ulster Constabulary. After initial training I was assigned to east Belfast where I worked in uniform duties. In 1968, I immigrated to Canada, where I joined the Metropolitan Toronto Police. After further training, I was assigned to 52 Division in downtown Toronto, where I performed uniform and plain clothes duties.

In 1978, I was promoted to sergeant and was transferred to the Morality Squad at police headquarters. I worked in several sections within the Morality Squad, finishing with a five-year stretch in the Drug Section. I was then promoted to staff sergeant and transferred to the training college, where I was an instructor and lecturer.

After two years at the police college, I was assigned to Internal Affairs, where my job was to investigate allegations of police corruption.

At no time was stress or Post Traumatic Stress Disorder part of the training for any of these positions. However, in my experience and from talking to individual officers, I would suggest PTSD is more prevalent than anyone would care to admit.

Officers who have had to kill or wound someone often turn to drink or drugs to dull the pain rather than seek help. The police mentality of "suck it up and move on" prevails.

One officer told me he almost had to kill someone. The man had two weapons and was waving them around. Luckily, he was talked down and no one was injured or killed. That was seven years ago, and that officer to this day is haunted by the memory of almost having to take a life. He has nightmares and can't sleep, but he is unwilling to ask for help.

Some officers who have left the job have spoken out about their problems, but Jimmy Bremner is one of the first active officers I know of who is willing to stand up and say how PTSD nearly ruined his life. He knows police officers involved in critical incidents need to know there is help and that they are not alone.

In my opinion, no police service has a good way to deal with critical incidents. Services may have readily available support but because it's not mandatory, officers are not willing to be centred out by seeking help.

In 1987, I was assigned to the Toronto Police Service's tactical team. The ETF selection process starts with a fitness test conducted at the police college physical fitness unit. Candidates who meet the criteria and pass the test are interviewed by members of the ETF management team. When interviewing and reviewing personnel files, the interviewers look for maturity, integrity, whether the candidate is a "team player," sick record and of course common sense. "Cowboys are not welcome." The last process is a psychological test and an interview by a psychologist. However, there is no follow-up with the psychologist in later years.

As a result of a number of high-profile calls I had been involved with, I was given the opportunity to share my experiences with other police services by way of being a guest lecturer, first at the Canadian Police College and later at conferences.

In the mid to late 1990s, I was subpoenaed to attend a number of inquests to testify about what crisis negotiators are taught and how police should conduct themselves at critical incidents. I realized that more training and continuous training was required, as was the help of mental health experts during some of these incidents. A group of crisis negotiators and I decided to form an association that would hold annual conferences, produce newsletters and conduct training to support the initial training by the Canadian Police College.

Upon my retirement from the Toronto Police Service in 2003, the association was incorporated. Canadian Critical Incident Inc. (CCII) continues to train in the area of incident command (hostage, barricade), crisis negotiations and incident command scribe training. The association produces three newsletters a year and hosts an annual fall conference dedicated to incident commanders, crisis negotiators, tactical officers and scribes for incident commanders.

CCII includes about 50 police services and correctional institutions, with members including crisis negotiators, incident commanders and tactical officers. The association has three mental health experts on its advisory board.

In 1996, as a result of recommendations from an inquest into the death of Troy Emmerson, an individual shot and killed by a member of the Ottawa Police Service, most tactical officers in Ontario now receive training in crisis negotiations. Interestingly, the Ontario Standards for Tactical Teams insist that there must be a selection process for tactical officers and a physical fitness test, *but* they require no psychological test, and certainly no ongoing psychological testing. It's up to the officer to seek help.

PTSD has been the subject of a number of articles in CCII newsletters and at our annual conferences. I also discuss it during incident command courses and crisis negotiators' courses, as do our mental health experts.

Most officers think when they seek help or advice from a psychiatrist or psychologist, there is a "stigma" involved. That's why I believe *all* officers involved in work that brings them in contact with critical incidents *must* see a mental health specialist for an assessment. The problem with this being a procedural mandate is that police associations worry that a negative finding would, or could, be used by management to jeopardize the officer's career.

During the last 20 years working in the field of critical incidents, I have spoken with numerous police officers who have been involved in police-related shooting fatalities. Unfortunately, the criteria used by police services during a post-shooting event vary immensely from service to service. For example, I recently spoke with an officer who, in 1995, shot and killed a suicidal subject who was armed with a firearm and was pointing it at the police, ignoring their repeated requests to drop the firearm. The subject started to walk in the direction of the officer, pointing his firearm at him and refusing to obey the officer's commands. The officer, fearing for the lives of his team members, and his own, had no alternative but to shoot and kill the subject.

I asked the officer how he felt he was treated by his supervisors and management after the shooting. He explained that he felt management and supervisors were very supportive. Psychological counselling was available but it was not mandatory. The officer went on to explain that the camaraderie and debriefings held with his fellow team members were the support he needed most. He went back to work the following day. This officer was also subject to the usual investigation by the civilian law enforcement agency Special Investigation Unit, which operates at arm's length from the Ontario Ministry of the Attorney General. The SIU's mission is to increase the confidence of all citizens of Ontario in their police services through professional and independent investigations of incidents involving police that have resulted in serious injury, including sexual assault or death. But for police officers, it can be a stressful time. I am happy to report that in this case, the officer worked through the trauma and is now an inspector with his police service.

In another incident, a police officer in Ontario was called to a scene where a male subject was holding a firearm to the head of a female hostage, who was seated beside the subject in the front of his vehicle. The subject was told to put the firearm down, which he refused to do, and consequently, fearing that the female's life was in danger, the officer shot and killed the subject, thereby saving the hostage's life.

The officer felt management was very supportive, but that they appeared to be more concerned with the "integrity" of the investigation than for the officer's well-being. He said while removing the subject from his vehicle, he was contaminated with the subject's blood. The officer was delayed from attending hospital for treatment, and in particular did not get the antiviral cocktail as soon as is normally recommended.

The officer was advised to take as much time off as he thought was necessary to recover from the incident. However, sitting at home alone watching press conferences held by his superiors on television, he felt isolated, and thought he would have been better off at work. Once again, psychological counselling was available but not mandatory and he chose not to seek help.

Officers who have shot people will always be subjected to the seizure of their firearm and all exterior clothing and equipment (for forensic purposes), and of course immediately be isolated from their fellow officers. You can envision what is going through their head. "I have just killed someone. I'm on my own, stripped of my uniform and gun, isolated and told a lawyer has been notified for me. I haven't done anything wrong. I just saved someone's life. Why am I being treated like this?"

I recently sent a survey to tactical teams in Ontario through the Ontario Tactical Advisory Board's email with respect to ongoing psychological assessments with tactical team members. The results were what I expected. Some teams have psychological testing for new members. None had ongoing psychological assessments for current members. Psychological assessments or counselling is available to all tactical team members but it is not mandatory.

We know that all human beings are different, and consequently, will react differently to similar situations, but I believe that "continuity and consistency" in these types of incidents by management is mandatory for the well-being of the police officers.

Education regarding PTSD should be part of the curriculum for police recruits and should then continue with in-service training. Officers in units dealing with extremely dangerous or extremely unpleasant situations (traffic investigators, child pornography investigators, undercover drug squad officers, tactical officers) on a regular basis, should, as part of their working conditions, be counselled, assessed and interviewed by professionals whose expertise is PTSD. This should be on an annual basis.

So how can we ensure that these officers get the treatment they might need? Here are some suggestions from Dr. Mini Mamak, a forensic psychologist at St. Joseph's Healthcare in Hamilton and assistant professor at McMaster University. She has taught courses with me at the Canadian Police College, internationally in Turkey, and is on the CCII advisory board.

•In a perfect world, police services would readily acknowledge that PTSD is a real and significant issue for officers and be proactive in providing treatment not only for PTSD, but also for the other mental health issues that can surface in response to trauma and even stress.

•Police services should be proactive in de-stigmatizing PTSD among its officers and should assist and support officers in receiving treatment. Ideally, treatment would be off-site and provided by qualified mental health professionals, who would work within a framework of confidentiality. Treatment would also be offered to family, to help them learn strategies to aid in the treatment of their loved ones and to address the impact PTSD has on the family constellation.

•In being proactive, in an ideal system, police services would also routinely screen those working in departments who are at the highest risk of developing PTSD (first responders, traffic). Yearly or bi-annual psychological evaluations/consultations may assist in identifying those who are struggling with PTSD or other mental health issues. Treatment consequently could be provided at the early stages of the disorder, thus reducing the likelihood that the condition becomes a chronic issue that has long-term implications for the individual with respect to job performance.

Organizations that could encourage this to happen are the provincial and Canadian governments, The Canadian Chiefs of Police Association, the Canadian Police Association and the Ontario Tactical Advisory Board.

An interesting article was published in *The FBI Law Enforcement Bulletin*, Sept. 1993. In his article, Michael D. Mashburn states that police administrators need to take a proactive approach when dealing with stress within their departments. They sometimes get involved only when they need to cure a problem, rather than attempting to prevent the problem.

Administrators can begin by instituting in-service training classes that better enable the officers to deal with Post Traumatic Stress when it occurs. While administrators cannot control all of life's events or the nature of criminal activity that turns to violence, they can take steps to educate officers to deal with them when they arise, Mr. Mashburn writes.

At CCII, we agree that support, whether by fellow officers, especially those who have been through traumatic experiences, or mental health professionals, is of utmost importance. It's also important that officers realize there is no stigma attached to reaching out for help and that being open and honest is part of the process to getting well. To make this happen, policies must be put in place.

After a critical incident, Ontario's correctional service department encourages its team members to have a briefing, which they call a "Post Traumatic Stress Experience." The correctional service managers believe getting together to discuss the incident will help prevent the experience from becoming PTSD. The police service should do the same.

Jimmy has been an inspiration and I have personally put him in contact with officers who have been involved in fatal shootings. Jimmy and Dr. Sean P. O'Brien have been to police services to talk about PTSD, particularly services that have had a number of police suicides. The Bremner/O'Brien team has also talked about PTSD at CCII's annual conferences. By sharing his story, Jimmy is fighting to dispel the stigma that asking for help equals weakness.

The time is right for Jimmy Bremner's book. There is currently a whole lot of discussion about PTSD, mostly in relation to war vets, but it's a subject that first responders, and especially those on tactical teams, need to educate themselves about and come to terms with. Pretending that there's nothing wrong is like hiding your head in the sand.

Just because officers are trained to take a life doesn't mean it's easy to do. It bothers anyone to take a life. You're not alone. It bothers anyone to see what we see on the job. You're not alone. Talk to someone. Ask for help. You're not alone.

13

"As my grandmother always used to say, there isn't anything that couldn't be worse."

The Last Word

When you're struggling through rough times, it's all about keeping the faith. Sometimes it's in the little moments that you find hope and inspiration for example, when a compassionate person takes the time to listen and sympathize with the events going on in another's life.

One particularly bad day, just a year ago, I was sitting in a coffee shop, and I guess I looked troubled. An elderly woman took the time to ask what was wrong. This simple, kind gesture went a long way toward restoring my spirits and hope. I left the conversation with a feeling of acceptance, and isn't that what we all want?

Surprisingly, compassionate people aren't hard to find if you are willing to share the experience, and positive encounters are always inspirational. It's OK to let down your guard. Ask for help and go to rehab. If I had not gone to rehab, there is a good chance I wouldn't be here to share my story.

New challenges and accomplishments serve to rebuild confidence. I started small and built up to doing the things I used to do, and used to enjoy doing. Every day is a victory and nothing builds hope like success.

Watching others' successful recovery from any of life's setbacks is inspirational. To that end, if my story inspires any of you to begin the journey back, helps you manage or avoid problems in the first place or simply offers hope, I am thankful.

There is hope and there is help. Just ask. As my grandmother always used to say, there isn't anything that couldn't be worse.

Jimmy's
Photo Album

Good use-of-force trainers drill officers repeatedly until responses become automatic.

The best way to be prepared for anything is to practice as many different scenarios as possible.

Knowing how to rappell and use distraction devices (bottom left) is part of the training.

I enjoy sharing my tactical knowledge, experience and personal insights with other officers.

Mike Babineau and I have shared experiences, both good and bad.

My wife, Dayle, has been with me through thick and thin.

My friend Dr. Sean P. O'Brien and I work together to educate officers about PTSD.

Barney McNeilly, president of Canadian Critical Incident Inc., is a constant source of support.

Being on the set of Flashpoint, *with Enrico Colantoni and the rest of the cast, has given me a sense of self beyond policing. With each new episode, I grow more confident.*

Actor Hugh Dillon and I hit it off immediately. Because we have both spent time in rehab, he knows what I'm talking about when I talk about my worst days.

I have shared my experiences with Flashpoint *co-creators Mark Ellis and Stephanie Morgenstern. They email me scripts and call me with technical questions about weapons and equipment.*

Flashpoint *writers Mark Ellis and Stephanie Morgenstern have said they would pass along my mantra – cops are trained to fire their weapon. They are not trained to kill people.*

I enjoy working when Flashpoint *is shooting on location. I'm shown here with (from left)* Flashpoint *co-creator Stephanie Morgenstern, actors Enrico Colantoni and Hugh Dillon, and executive producer Anne Marie La Traverse.*

Amy Jo Johnson, Enrico Colantoni, Hugh Dillon, David Paetkau, Michael Cram and Sergio Di Zio portray members of the fictional Strategic Response Unit on Flashpoint. *I have offered tactical training to the actors and consider them my team.*

I first thought about writing a book when I was in rehab. Who would have thought it would actually happen? These photos are from my first book cover photo shoot. My co-author, Connie Adair, joins me in a photo.

Acknowledgments

Make no mistake, I could not have made the turnaround on my own. There have been special people along the way – my wife, Dayle, being number one and my kids second – my son, Michael, for his cool head and my daughter, Kacey, for her fighting spirit. And there are my teammates who stuck by my side and checked in on my family when I could not.

Thanks also to the people who took the time to listen and not judge – those who believed in me and knew I still had worth, even when I didn't believe in myself. I would like to name each of you but I'm not sure if you would appreciate it because many of you are still active members. But you know who you are – a teammate who is like a brother, a mentor, a father, a kindred spirit. At my best, at my worst you were by my side. Through the transformation you listened to me at length no matter what time of day or night, offering unconditional acceptance, non-judgmental, only giving advice when asked. You spent time with me when you had other things to do, never rushing to leave, and you stood up to the non-believers. You had the courage to stand by my side even if it affected the way people viewed you. You were strong enough to show your tender side – the mark of a true warrior and the mark of a compassionate human being.

While in recovery it occurred to me that PTSD and the impact it had on police officers and their families was little understood. I knew it was time for me to became a crusader for trauma victims. As part of my therapy I kept a journal, which became the seed of *Crack in the Armor.*

Acknowledgments

I could not have completed this book without the help of many. I would like to extend my thanks to Sean O'Brien, Mike Babineau, Barney McNeilly, Mark Ellis and Stephanie Morgenstern for their contributions to the book. I would especially like to thank my wife, Dayle. It was emotionally difficult for her to relive the tough times. She perservered in the hope that she could help other families.

Thank you to Connie Adair for putting my feelings into words. Thanks also to the Truongs for their striking book cover design, and to Donald G. Bastian for his editorial and publishing advice.

Flashpoint photos pages 144, 145 top and 147 by Michael Gibson.
Photos pages 142 bottom, 148, 149 and 150 by Marko Shark.

Contributors

Mike Babineau
Sgt., retired

Mike Babineau is retired from policing and is under contract to take part in the development of course training standards as well as designing, delivering and evaluating training for the newly formed Nuclear Swat Teams.

Prior to this assignment, Mike served for 35 years with the Toronto Police Service. He retired in May 2008, having attained the rank of sergeant.

From late 2000 until his retirement, Mike was the senior firearms instructor for the service and administrative assistant to the armament officer and as such was responsible for developing and delivering firearms training and tactical training exercises for all members of his police service.

Mike also served a number of years with SWAT as a gun team sergeant. In this capacity he participated in the resolution of more than 185 high-risk incidents, including gun and offensive weapons calls, hostage and barricaded person situations and high-risk warrant service. Mike also has 22 years of experience performing general police duties, including various uniform and investigative assignments.

Mike is the recipient of several awards, including the Canadian Police Exemplary Service Medal and Bar. He is the recipient of two commendations from the Chief of Police, as well as 37 letters of commendation.

Mark Ellis and Stephanie Morgenstern

Mark Ellis is the co-creator and co-executive producer of the hit drama *Flashpoint*, which airs on CBS, CTV and networks around the world. The series has earned 34 Gemini nominations to date, including a best writing nod for Mark and co-writer Stephanie Morgenstern, and best dramatic series.

Mark and Stephanie co-wrote and starred in the acclaimed short film *Remembrance*, which Stephanie directed. It won a Jutra Award, a Genie nomination and top prize at the Worldwide Short Film Festival. A feature film version has been optioned.

Ellis's acting credits include leading and support roles in television and film. He also worked extensively at theatres across the country, most recently in *2 Pianos 4 Hands*.

Mark has lectured about writing for television and short film in Canada and Europe. He attended Ryerson University's Radio and Television Arts program and the Berlinale Talent Campus.

Stephanie Morgenstern is an award-winning actor, screenwriter and filmmaker and both a Genie and Gemini nominee. She was designated National Indie Treasure by Toronto's *EYEWEEKLY*, profiled in *Voir magazine* as a New Face to Watch and selected as one of three Great Expectations filmmakers at the Telluride International Film Festival in Colorado.

Contributors

Stephanie began her career as a professional actor at the age of 15 in Montreal, working in English and French. Feature film highlights include *The Sweet Hereafter, Maelstrom* and *Revoir Julie*. Stephanie studied acting at the Banff Centre for the Arts, holds a BA in English from McGill University and an MA in Social and Political Thought from York University, and is an alumna of both the Berlinale Talent Campus and of the Women in the Director's Chair Master Class.

Stephanie and her partner Mark Ellis are co-creators and co-executive producers of the CTV/CBS drama *Flashpoint*, winner of the Gemini award for Best Dramatic Series. They earned Gemini and Writers Guild nominations as well as two Prism Award commendations for their work on the show. Stephanie also played a cameo role as the hostage in *Flashpoint's* pilot episode, "Scorpio."

Barney McNeilly
S/Sgt., retired

A senior law enforcement professional with over 35 years of policing experience in uniform, investigative and management functions in Northern Ireland and Canada, Barney recently retired from the Toronto Police Service.

Barney provides consulting services for continuing education to members of the law enforcement community. He is founder and current president of Canadian Critical Incident Incorporated, an association that hosts annual conferences across Canada for commanders, negotiators and tactical officers.

He was second in charge of the Toronto Police Emergency Task Force, one of the busiest tactical teams in North America. He was recognized as the chief crisis negotiator for the Toronto Police Service and was involved in the successful resolution of over 200 hostage/barricaded incidents. Barney has also observed and participated in critical incident programs of Scotland Yard and FBI Quantico.

Lecturing on behalf of the Canadian Police College for the past 15 years, Barney has testified at a number of coroner's inquests as an expert witness in the area of incident command and crisis negotiations with respect to hostage/barricaded incidents.

Barney has travelled internationally, conducting courses and exercises in Colombia, United Arab Emirates, Barbados, St. Lucia, Grenada, Antigua, Argentina and Turkey.

Contributors

At the request of the Bermuda Police Service, Barney travelled to Bermuda where he conducted an investigation of the use of force by members of its tactical team. He has also completed similar investigations on behalf of the cities of Vancouver and Thunder Bay and on behalf of An Garda Siochana Tactical Unit, Ireland.

Dr. Sean P. O'Brien

Dr. Sean P. O'Brien is a registered clinical psychologist who currently maintains a private practice in the Toronto area. The majority of his work involves the provision of clinical and consultation services to policing and government organizations throughout North America, including the Toronto and Durham Regional police services, the RCMP, the U.S. Marshals Service and the United Nations.

Dr. O'Brien has more than 15 years of experience dealing with high-profile critical incidents, including police shootings, criminal investigations into police conduct, serious criminal activities and terrorism and war-related events. He works with various agencies to demystify the Post Traumatic Stress response and to develop strategies to help police officers and military personnel reduce their risk of developing a Post Traumatic Stress Disorder.

Dr. O'Brien is also a use-of-force consultant to various government agencies, police services and private security contractors throughout Canada and the United States.

Bibliography

American Psychiatric Association. (2000). *Diagnostic and statistical manual of mental disorders (4th ed., text revision)*. Washington, DC.

Cunningham, A. (2002) *The healing journey: Overcoming the crisis of cancer*. Toronto: Key Porter Books.

Fairbank J.A., Ebert, L. and Caddell, J.M. (2001) *Post traumatic stress disorder*. In P.B. Sutker and H.E. Adams (Eds.), *Comprehensive handbook of psychopathology* (pp.183-209). New York: Kluwer Academic/Plenum Publishers.

Foa, E. and Rothbaum, B.O. (1998) *Treating the trauma of rape*. New York: Guilford Press.

Grossman, D. (2008). *On combat: The psychology and physiology of deadly conflict in war and peace*. Millstadt: Warrior Science Publications.

Herman, J. (1997). *Trauma and recovery: the aftermath of violence – from domestic abuse to political terror*. New York: Basic Books.

Hole, J.W. (2001). *Human anatomy and physiology*. Dubuque: Wm. C. Brown.

Laur, Darren (2002). *The anatomy of fear and how it relates to survival skills training*. Portland: LWC Books/Integrated Street Combatives.

Lewis, C. (2004, Sept.). *Police suicide is an alarming problem rarely discussed publicly. Tears of a cop website. Retrieved June 28, 2010 from www.tearsofacop.com.*

Mashburn, Michael D. (1993). *Critical incident counseling – importance of counseling for police officers. The FBI Law Enforcement Bulletin* (Sept. 1993).

Bibliography

McNally, R.J. (1999). *Post traumatic stress disorder.* In T. Millon, P.H. Blaney and R.D. Davis (Eds.), *Oxford Textbook of Psychopathology,* pp. 144-165. New York: Oxford University Press.

Siddle, K. (2006) *Bio-psychological responses to simulated firearms events.* Paper presented to PPCT Management Systems.

Siddle, K. and Grossman, D. (1998). *Effects of hormonal induced heart rate increase. Post Traumatic Gazette,* 4(4), pp. 6-7.

Turvey, B. (1995). *Police officers: control, hopelessness and suicide.* Knowledge Solutions Library, Electronic Publication, URL: http:/www.corpus-delicti.com/suicide.html (April 1995).

Index

About the Authors

Jimmy Bremner has over 24 years of experience in law enforcement. He has served in uniform patrol, SWAT (as a gun team member, team leader, sniper, rappel master, explosives technician and Gun-Gang Task Force (weapons technician and tactical trainer), and is currently assigned as a Use of Force and Firearms instructor. Jimmy can be reached at jim.bremner@gmail.com or james@bremnerassociates.com

About the Authors

Connie Adair is a feature writer based in Toronto. She is a regular contributor to the *National Post* and *Post Homes Magazine*, and has written feature articles for many consumer and business publications, including *More, Glow, Homes & Cottages, REM: The Real Estate Magazine, The Toronto Star* and *The Toronto Sun*. She has also written for television and corporate communications projects. Prior to her freelance writing career, she spent several years as a writer and editor at the Toronto Real Estate Board. Connie lives with her husband, Jim, and sons, Alex and Adam. Connie can be reached at cadair@pathcom.com

Want a copy of this book for yourself, a friend or colleague,
or a bulk order for your workplace?
Visit **www.bremnerassociates.com**